A People's History of

Prince Edward Island

Steel Rail Publishing
P.O. Box 6813, Station A
TORONTO, Ontario
M5W 1X6

Typeset by Zeus Phototype
Printed by Web Offset

A People's History

of

Prince Edward Island.

Errol Sharpe

Steel Rail Publishing
Toronto, 1976

Steel Rail Publishing

Publishing for the People

The main thrust of Steel Rail Publishing is to search for and
publish books written by Canadians about the Canadian people's
struggles throughout their history. We shall also publish international materials of interest to the Canadian people in their
struggle for an independent socialist Canada.

Steel Rail Publishing is a house through which people can exchange ideas and publish materials that might not otherwise be
published.

Canadian Cataloguing in Publication Data

Sharpe, Errol, 1940-
    A people's history of Prince Edward Island

Bibliography: p.
Includes index.

ISBN 0-88791-003-3 bd.   ISBN 0-88791-001-7 pa.

1. Prince Edward Island - History. I. Title.

FC2611.S43   971.7   C76-017075-4
F1048.S43

Contents

Introduction

History is made by people. History is the story of the struggles of the people, their victories in their countries and communities, their mistakes, their creations, their downfalls and their aspirations.

But most often this is not what we are taught when we study history. We learn of kings, governors, members of parliament, and premiers and the role they play in governing our lives. The stories of the governed are left untold.

In modern countries, capitalist societies, which are divided into classes, history is made by the struggle between classes.

This book does not try to be neutral.

It frankly tells the history of the Island from a people's perspective. It explains how the tenant farmers, the independent merchants, the fishermen, workers and farmers fought to improve their conditions and improve their society.

The ultimate victory in all people's struggles is the end of class society and equality among the people. The pages of this book discuss how these struggles have been carried out in the past, are being carried out in the present and will continue in the future.

This book would not have been possible without the help and encouragement of many people. I wish to thank particularly the following who have been of special assistance:

1) The staff at the Public Archives of Canada, The Public Archives of Prince Edward Island, The University of Prince Edward

Island Library, The Confederation Centre Library in Charlotte-town and the Metropolitan Toronto Central Library. All have been most helpful in assisting this amateur researcher.

2) Art Gormley and members of the Labourers' Protective Union, Charlottetown, Bertram Blaquiere, Rustico, Theophilus Blanchard, North Rustico, Leo Dowling, Charlottetown, Mr. and Mrs. Burke, Bay Fortune, and the Lalacheur family of Guernsey Cove, all of whom responded to requests for information and answered many questions in a spirit of co-operation and helpfulness. Without their vivid accounts of personal experiences many of the more interesting and informative aspects of the people's history would have remained hidden.

3) Kent Martin, Kerstin Martin, Brian Pollard, Harry Holman, Gary Webster, Jim Kelly, Ian Robertson, Milton Acorn and many others who willingly shared their own personal knowledge, made suggestions and corrected errors.

4) Edith Hemery, Olino Capacchione, Linda Capacchione, Greg Keilty, Peter Davies, Marjorie Robertson, Denise Havers, Hazel Zinkiev and others who helped in typing manuscript, editing, proof reading, lay-out, design, typesetting, etc.

5) Finally, I would like to say an extra special thanks to my wife Susan, my father Lindsay Sharpe, brothers and sister and the people of Norboro, for without their help, understanding and patience, this work would have been much more difficult, if not impossible.

I gratefully acknowledge the financial assistance of the Canada Council and the Ontario Arts Council which made the writing of this book possible.

Errol Sharpe
Toronto
July 1976

1

The first people

The first Europeans to settle permanently in North America came a little more than four hundred years ago. They came twenty five thousand years after the first inhabitants had migrated from Asia over the land bridge that then existed between Siberia and Alaska. Fifteen thousand years passed before the descendants of these migrants reached present-day Prince Edward Island yet their arrival on the island preceded that of the Europeans by some ten thousand years. Indeed, those first Islanders didn't even live on an island. At that time Prince Edward Island was connected to the mainland by a land bridge. The route they took is marked today by the red sandy shore of Cape Tormentine in New Brunswick and the red sandstone cliffs that rise out of the sea across the Northumberland Strait at Borden, Prince Edward Island.

Archaeologists call these first Islanders "Paleo-Indians". The native people of Canada and the rest of the Americas have all been called Indians since Christopher Columbus, in 1492, mistakenly thought he had landed in India. Thus the first settlers of these continents, although they had evolved during their thousands of years here into many different and distinct linguistic and cultural groups, were all stereotyped. The Europeans' ignorance of and contempt for the native people destroyed their culture and provided an excuse for the theft of their lands. By branding them savages they justified their treatment of the first inhabitants. The English called them "red men" because the first natives they encountered were the Beothuk of Newfoundland whose custom it was to colour their skin with a red ochre.

The common lot of all the native peoples of Eastern Canada was the unending struggle to fulfil their basic economic needs of food, clothing and shelter. In the hostile environment in which they lived, all had to participate in this struggle. There was no surplus to allow an elite to live off the labour of others. Everything was shared, people worked together and private property did not exist.

Little is known about the Paleo people except that they lived through fishing, hunting and gathering plants. Their main hunting and fishing weapon was the spear. No record of the name by which they identified their homeland has survived.

About three thousand years ago the Paleo were conquered by a new people who moved in from the south. The cultures of the two groups were combined. The best and most useful tools and customs of each were integrated so that a richer and more diversified society emerged. The newcomers' staple diet was shellfish, therefore archaeologists have called them the "Shellfish People". In recent years, numerous shell heaps called *middens* have been discovered along the north shore of the Island, marking the sites of their camps.

Shellfish were not their only food supply. Although they had not learned how to use salt to cure fish, they did smoke clams and oysters to preserve them for winter use. Their menu possibly consisted of as many as thirty different kinds of birds, berries and other wild plants.

Two thousand years ago, still sixteen hundred years before the arrival of the white man, a group of eastern Algonkians moved into the Maritimes from what is now central Canada.

The Shellfish People's men were killed in battle and the women and children were adopted. The new people, who called themselves *Micmac*, occupied the sites of the Shellfish People and used whatever of their tools they found useful. Eventually intermarriage and integration of the two cultures produced a new people and culture, neither Algonkian nor Shellfish. It was a com-

Dug Out Canoe: *The Micmac selected a large tree, cut it down to the shape they wanted, then lit a fire to burn out the centre, which was then also finished with an axe. The Dug Out was the earliest canoe used before they had learned to make the much lighter and more mobile birch bark canoe. (Public Archives, P.E.I.—PAPEI).*

Micmac and Tepee: *When on summer trips the Micmac still use a tepee. While this tepee is covered with canvas, the original tepee was covered with skins. The original tepee might also be much larger than the one pictured. Their size depended on the size of the individual family. (PA-PEI).*

bination of parts of both with its own unique features.

The Micmac

The Micmac gave the Island its first recorded names, *Minagoo*, meaning simply "the Island", and the more romantic *Abewait*, meaning "Cradled on the Waves". Present-day inhabitants still prefer the name "The Island", reserving the legal title, Prince Edward Island, for official and formal purposes.

In the days of the greatest flourishing of the Micmac, Minagoo was a land covered with rich forests sheltering clear rivers flowing to sea swept beaches. The rivers abounded with fish, the forests with game and the beaches with shellfish. The Micmac used all of these for food. Their communal campsites are still marked by "Indian Orchards" where small clumps of fruit trees and berry bushes sprang from the seeds they tossed aside many years ago.

The Micmac lived in harmony with nature. Early settlers described them as a happy and humane people. Many missionaries and explorers owed their lives to the Micmacs' benevolence, compassion and ability to survive in the natural environment.

Each year brought the relative plenty of summer and the threat of starvation in winter when it took the combined effort of the whole band to provide food. In January, the chief source of food was the winter stores of smoked fish and such fresh game as the hunter could catch. A great delicacy was the seal which provided not only food but oil used year round as a kind of sauce. In spring they caught the fish which headed up stream to spawn. The return of the birds and spring eggs provided welcome relief from the winter diet. Summer also brought a great variety of fish, shellfish, roots, fresh game and berries.

In summer the Micmac gathered in large camps along the north shore of Minagoo at places with names like *Kaskamkek*, "bold sandy shore" (Cascumpec), *Makpaak*, "big bay" (Malpeque), *Kicheboogwek Booktaba*, "bay of shoals" (New London), *Tabooetooetun* "having two outlets (Rustico), *Tilakadik*, "camping ground" (Tracadie) and *Kadotpichk* "eel water place" (Savage Harbour). [1]

Their homes, called wigwams, were placed in long rows by the water's edge. They had time for social life, storytelling, courtship and games. These ancient traditions are remembered to this day when the Island Micmac gather on Lennox Island to celebrate the feast of St Anne.

In late September and early October they left the beaches to prepare for winter. Those who came across the strait to this summer camping ground braved the rough autumn waters to return to the richer winter hunting grounds of the mainland. Those who remained turned inland in family groups to set up their winter camps. As the supply of fish and small game was depleted, the camps were moved to new locations. Success of the hunt meant food for the camps, failure meant hunger for all.

The Micmac required few political structures, relying almost exclusively on their customs and public opinion. Survival required strict rules to regulate life in the closely knit communities. Each had his role and each role was respected. Brother respected sister and was careful not to speak out rudely in a sister's presence. A man would not enter the wigwam of a woman whose husband was not present nor would a woman enter the wigwam of a man whose wife was not present. Violators of the Micmac codes were sometimes dealt with by the chief but more often the offender was turned over to the offended.

Usually if he repented and made amends he was forgiven. Harsher treatment was reserved for those who committed acts which threatened the community. In such a case the offender faced expulsion or complete ostracism. One so punished was usually cast into the forest, homeless and friendless where he was the prey of wild animals and evil spirits. In the harsh climate a person alone could not survive long. Even when allowed to remain in the camp ostracism by the group usually drove him to insanity.

Micmac religion centred around worship of the sun, the giver of warmth and life. Lesser deities included *Shadegomutc*, an evil spirit, and *Gluscap*, a good spirit, the father and giver of many gifts to his people. Some living people were *ginap*, possessors of great strength and endurance used for good.

Children were showered with tenderness and affection by the whole family. During the day the very young were wrapped in furs and carried in cradleboards strapped to their mothers' backs so the women could continue their work. When the babies cried, mothers would dance and sing a lullaby as they continued their task. Soft moss or sea weed served as diapers in the cradleboard packs. Much of the Micmac's art and decorative design appeared on the clothing of the children. Fathers carved toys for their infants out of wood and stone.

Preparation for marriage was an important part of a young Micmac's life. When a young man wished to court a young woman he gave gifts to her father. To show any affection, even to look at her, would make him the laughing stock of the community. If the young woman was interested in the advances of her suitor a meeting of relatives would be arranged to discuss the marriage. If this meeting went well the young man would live in the wigwam of the young woman's parents, often for as long as a year. If all proved satisfactory and the young man was considered suitable, the couple then married and raised their own family.

In Micmac society, the division of labour was according to sex, not class as it is today. The roles played by men and women in the constant search for food were strictly adhered to, and were largely determined by the conditions imposed by nature. The women, charged with the care of the children, stayed at home. Here they made utensils out of bark and clay, dug clams, picked berries, cooked the meals and made clothing for their families. The men were the hunters and the warriors. When it came time to move, the women took down the wigwams and carried them and everything else to the new encampment allowing the men to go ahead to break the trail.

In the late fifteenth and early sixteenth centuries the communal life of the Micmac and their brothers and sisters in eastern Canada was disrupted and later destroyed by the arrival of the white man. It was the native people who were to provide most of the labour which produced the furs and other riches upon which the colonial empires of the Europeans were built. As the Micmac devoted more and more time to trapping and working for the white man, and buying their necessities from him, they spent less and less time pursuing their traditional way of life. By the mid-seventeenth century, Micmac society had altered to the extent that stone tools were no longer made. They had become dependent on the white man. When they were no longer needed to trap fur-bearing animals they were unable to return to their traditional ways. Their land was occupied and they had forgotten the ancient skills of survival.

Since those days, three hundred years ago, the Micmac have been living in limbo. Neither returning to their ancient ways nor assimilating fully into the society of the Europeans, they were cast aside onto reserves where they became dependent on the demeaning and graceless "charity" of government welfare. But today, they are on the move. In growing unity native people across North America are organising to reassert their rightful place in these, their native lands.

Chapter Notes

1. Alan Rayburn, *Geographical Names of Prince Edward Island*, Ottawa, Dept. of Energy, Mines and Resources, 1973, Alphabetical listings.
* See also: John H. Maloney, "And in the Beginning ..." in Francis W.P. Bolger (ed.), *Canada's Smallest Province: A History of Prince Edward Island*, Charlottetown, Centennial Commission, 1973.

2

The first Europeans

The Conquerors

On June 30, 1534, the inhabitants of Minagoo watched a small sailing ship enter what is today Malpeque Bay.

The ship carried Jacques Cartier, sent by Francis I, king of France, in search of a sea route to China. He had sailed into the Gulf of St Lawrence thinking that this inland sea would lead him there.

Cartier was not the first European to visit Minagoo. Before him, fishermen working for Spanish, Portuguese, French and English merchants came to the rich fishing grounds of eastern Canada. The men pulled the fish from the teeming sea, piled them on the decks of their small ships to be cleaned and later took them ashore to be dried in the summer sun. Although they left no permanent settlements they did establish fish stations in secluded harbours to which they returned year after year.

In the fisheries, the merchants arranged matters to their advantage. Since fishermen received a share of their catch as their wage, they bore the proud title of co-adventurers. However, they did not share equally with the merchants in the benefits of the industry. The merchants set the cost of provisions high and the price at which they bought the fish low. Thus, the fishermen who laboured at a risk to their very lives were in the grip of the profiteering merchants. (More than 400 years later, little has changed.)

Even the fishermen were not the first Europeans to reach North America and perhaps even the shores of Minagoo. In the 11th and 12th centuries, the Vikings from Scandinavia established colonies in Greenland and Newfoundland. Medieval legends attribute even earlier voyages to "islands of the west" to Irish and Welsh seafarers.

Because the fishermen were not of the social class that received the attention of contemporary writers no record of their experiences was made. The stories of their voyages were passed down by word of mouth from generation to generation—stories of an Isle St Jean or St John's Island. It was the fishermen who gave Minagoo its first European name.

Cartier was the first European to leave a written record of Minagoo. He called the bay *Rivière des Barques* (Malpeque) when he saw Micmac crossing the water. Later that same day he sighted North Cape which he named *Cap des Sauvages*. Cartier never knew that he had seen an island but his description of it is rich and colourful.

> That day we coasted this shore some nine or ten leagues to try and find a harbour, but could not do so; for as I have already mentioned, the shore is low and the water shallow. We landed that day in four places to see the trees which were wonderfully beautiful and very fragrant. We discovered that that there were cedars, yaw-trees, pines, white elms, ash trees, willows and others, many of them unknown to us and all trees without fruit. The soil where there are no trees is also very rich and is covered with pease, white and red gooseberry bushes, strawberries, raspberries and wild oats like rye, which one would say had been sown there and tilled. It is the best tempered region one can possibly see and the heat is considerable. There are many turtle-doves, wood-pigeons and other birds. Nothing is wanting but harbours.[1]

Cartier and other explorers like him represented a new class in Europe, the merchants or bourgeois who were challenging feudalism which had dominated Europe for almost 1000 years.

The threat to the feudal system was marked by the growth of the town bourgeoisie ("burgers") and by the serf uprisings in the countryside. The chief benefactors of the new era were the merchants who began to trade, first locally and later with neighbouring towns and countries. It was the merchants, and the European monarchs financed by the merchants, who sent explorers west across the ocean in search of India and China and their gold and spices. They found the "new world".

The new economic order was *mercantilism*; the trading of goods for money. Harold Innis, a Canadian economist, has described the European centres from which the merchants operated as the "Metropolis" and the territory from which the resources were gathered as the "Hinterland". The centre of economic, political and cultural power was in the metropolis. There the merchants made the decisions which determined the economy of the hinterland.

Because there was no need for a large population to extract the raw materials from the hinterland, the merchants discouraged settlement. The settlement obligations written into the charters granted to merchant companies by the kings were ignored. Consequently, some charters were revoked for non-compliance of the obligation to etablish settlements.

The kings wanted settlements to solidify their claims to the new territories and to establish territorial boundaries. However, since the merchants not the kings ran affairs in the hinterland, their own well-being was paramount, not that of distant monarchs. For this reason, and in spite of much economic activity in the fur trade and fishing, the population of the Canadian hinterland remained small.

Colonies were established by French companies on the Bay of Fundy in Acadie (named Nova Scotia by the British in 1631) and on the shores of the St Lawrence River. The English did the same on the Atlantic coast farther south.

The French and English merchants wanted to expand trade by controlling as much as they could of the rich fur country. The best way to do this was to enlist the support of the native peoples. They were persuaded, by the merchants' agents, to hunt animals and prepare the furs in return for bits of mirror, common tools and alcohol. By enticing the natives to work for them, the Europeans destroyed their cultures and economies making them dependent on the Europeans for survival.

L'Acadie: 1701 French map. Note the almost total absence of names on Isle St Jean. (PAC).

The French made friends with the Algonquin, Micmac, Montagnais and Huron, the English with the Iroquois. The two European powers provoked the native peoples into fighting against each other, weakening themselves still further and making easier the exploitation of the hinterlands. Thus, in the name of Christian civilization were greed and oppression brought to North America.

La Compagnie de la Nouvelle France

After Port Royal was founded by Samuel de Champlain on the Bay of Fundy in 1605, Québec City (1608) and Montréal (1639) were established as the headquarters for the fur trade by *La Compagnie de la Nouvelle France.*

It was not until about 1650 that La Compagnie de la Nouvelle France expanded its operations to the fishing industry. Louix XIV of France granted new charters which included the right to fish on the rich fishing banks of the Atlantic Coast and in the Gulf of St Lawrence. The land bordering on these waters was given as a bonus to the merchant company.

In 1654, Nicholas Denys, an associate of La Compagnie de la Nouvelle France was made governor of a grant which included "all the country, territory, coasts and confines of the Great Bay of Saint Laurens, to commence with *Cap de Canceaux* (Canso) as far as the *Cap des Rosiers* (Gaspé), *Isles de Terre-Neufe* (Newfoundland), *Isles de Cap-Breton*, de *Saint-Jean* and other islands adjacent."[2] This territory provided France with an outer ring of defense against the British with whom they were almost continually at war.

Denys established a settlement on Ile de Cap-Breton as the headquarters for the fishing, fur trading, lumbering and mining operations. (He was the first to mine coal in Cape Breton). The Micmac provided the furs and French colonists, mostly prisoners from French jails, did all the other productive work.

Denys, like most of his contemporaries, was only interested in the profits to be extracted from the hinterland and did little to fulfil the settlement requirements of his grant. Therefore, in 1663, he lost the lucrative fishing rights to another associate of La Compagnie de la Nouvelle France, François Dublet. In 1667, yet

Fish Camp: *Artist Gerard Edema's conception of a fishing station in Placentia Bay, Newfoundland, about 1690. Similar camps were set up in many locations in the Maritime region by European fishermen. (Sigmund Samuel Canadiana Collection, Royal Ontario Museum, Toronto.)*

another associate, Sr de la Giraudiere, captured Denys' settlement. In the colonial hinterland, competing associates of the same company fought among themselves like feudal landlords for control of territory. In this case La Compagnie de la Nouvelle France arbitrated in favor of Denys but then revoked his grant completely in 1669.

Ile St Jean was included in other grants in the 1600's. Each grantee would make the pretence of encouraging settlement. None did. When the time came to revoke a grant and give the privileges to another favorite, the company's or the king's customary reason for changing the grantees would be that the previous grantee had not made settlements. There was no need to check. It was always true.

Emerging Empires

In England, by the middle of the 17th century, the bourgeoisie (merchants) had gained power.

In 1628, parliament, which the merchants controlled, forced

Charles I to sign the "Petition of Right" which would prevent him from raising money through taxes without permission of parliament. In 1642, civil war broke out between the bourgeoisie, led by Oliver Cromwell, and the feudal aristocracy, led by Charles I. Charles' armies were defeated and he was beheaded.

The new ruling class in the English metropolis accelerated resource extraction from the colonial hinterland. While the merchants did not allow manufacturing to develop in the hinterland, the North American colonies became important sources of foodstuffs as well as furs. Considerable settlement was necessary to develop agriculture. The great majority of the settlers came from the poor and starving people of Scotland and Ireland whose lands had been confiscated by the English conquerors to form large pastures, called "enclosures" used for sheep farming. Others came to escape religious persecution.

In 1650, France was still a feudal kingdom. Its merchant class was neither strong enough nor sufficiently well organised to seize power. As they were interested only in furs and fish, settlement in the French colonies, being unnecessary and expensive, was discouraged. As a result, that country's hinterland, New France, had a population of only 18,500 in 1715; the population of New England was 434,000.

From the outbreak of the Thirty Years War (1618-1648) for nearly a century, England and France were almost continually at war. Every clash between the two European powers was carried into North America. The regions on the ill-defined borders changed hands many times. Battles were fought on the high seas where, by 1650 on the fishing banks of eastern North America, France had 400 and England 300 vessels employing 18,000 and 15,000 men respectively.

Acadie was captured by the English and recaptured or returned to the French more than half a dozen times between 1613 and 1713.

Throughout the whole period of this power struggle, the people of Acadie were building their own communities in the wilderness. The first settlers came to Acadie with Champlain in 1605 and were soon joined by others from France, England, Spain, the Basque region and other parts of Europe. They came to the settle-

L'Acadie: *Later map (circa 1750) after the founding of Louisbourg and Halifax. By this time there were a number of French settlements and many more place names on Isle St Jean. (PAPEI).*

ment at Port Royal, to Minus Basin and to the Isthmus of Chignecto, where they farmed the rich marshlands and fished in the coastal waters. By 1700 the population had reached 2,000.

Isolated from France and descended from many different national backgrounds, the Acadiens were determined to build their own national identity. By 1700 they were a nation distinct from France and the French colonies on the St Lawrence. They had an economy that met their needs rather than the exploitive interests of the merchants. The King of France could grant their lands to successive merchant barons, could cancel the grants, and grant them again as he wished; it mattered little to the Acadiens, whose name came from the native word Akad, meaning "the People". The Acadiens, many with native blood, were the people of the place. French noblemen and later Englishmen adventurers could come and go; the people hardly knew their names.

In 1701, Louis XIV of France claimed the throne of Spain through inheritance. His action sparked the War of Spanish Succession. England entered the war to prevent France from taking over the Spanish Empire. In North America, where the war was called Queen Anne's War, Acadie fell into the permanent hands of the English in 1710. The Treaty of Utrecht, in 1713, officially ceded Acadie, Newfoundland and the Hudson Bay territory to the English: the French retained Cape Breton Island, Ile St Jean and Canada (New France).

Cape Breton, renamed Ile Royale, and Ile St Jean suddenly became strategically important to the French. The mighty fortress of Louisbourg was built in 1720 on the Atlantic coast of Ile Royal to protect the Atlantic fisheries and the route to Canada. Ile St Jean was to be developed to provide food for Louisbourg.

The Acadiens were caught more than ever in the struggle between the two imperial powers. The English demanded that they sign an Oath of Allegiance to the English king; they refused. Although they wanted to preserve their land and national identity, they would not take up arms against the French or their friends, the Micmac, who were allies of the French. Eventually, they were persuaded to sign an Oath of Fidelity binding them to remain neutral in the struggle between the European rivals, a solution which was satisfactory neither to the French nor to the English.

Chapter Notes

1. D.C.Harvey, *The French Regime in Prince Edward Island*, New Haven, Yale, 1926. pp 5-6.
2. *Ibid.*, p. 19.

3

The French régime

Breadbasket for Louisbourg

Louisbourg, the mightiest fortress in the "New World" became known as the Gibraltar of North America. It was "built on a narrow headland with water on three sides, the sea itself provided a moat and nine days out of ten the surf landed hard on the rock strewn shore. A string of shoals and islands that reduced the harbour entrance to a mere four hundred yards offered gun emplacements to command the roadstead and the only channel. The landward side was so marshy that it would surely swallow any heavy artillery an enemy might try to drag on to the low hillocks that lifted half a mile away."[1]

The walls were built of concrete ten feet thick and rose for thirty feet behind a steep ditch. There were 148 gun emplacements enabling either all-round fire, or a massive concentration at danger points. The population of Louisbourg was to reach 10,000 before its walls came tumbling down.

As early as 1716, the French made their first effort to develop agriculture on Ile St Jean. They persuaded a number of Acadiens to move from their English-held lands at Minus Basin to Ile St Jean. The Acadiens arrived only to find that a strip along the whole east coast a league wide (about three miles) had been granted to Sr de Louvigny, the mayor of Québec City. Those who found open marshland like that in Acadie along the Hillsborough

River remained: those who didn't returned in disgust to Acadie, preferring English mercantilism to French feudalism.

Subsequently, de Louvigny's grant was revoked and turned over to Comte de Saint Pierre, First Equerry to the Duchess of Orleans, whose husband was the regent of France before Louis XI came of age. In return for the grant St Pierre was to acknowledge homage to Louisbourg, without dues, and to bring 200 new settlers in the first year.

The first settlers arrived in 1720 and established Port La Joye on the west side of the present Charlottetown harbour. The new settlers held land under feudal tenure, paying rent to St Pierre.

St Pierre, like other merchants before him, was interested only in the money to be made from the fisheries. After the first year he refused to spend any more to bring settlers from France. The Acadiens, the Micmac and the few settlers who did come provided the labour for St Pierre's new fishing station, Havre St Pierre, named after himself, and the satellite ports of Havre à l'Anguille (Savage Harbour), Tracadie, Malpeque and Pointe Rouge (East Point).

In 1724, St Pierre deserted the colony; his profits weren't high enough. The next year his fishing rights were revoked. Nevertheless, it was through his efforts that the first permanent settlement was built.

By insisting on feudalism and thereby keeping away the Acadiens, the French delayed settlement and weakened their position in North America. Supplies for Louisbourg had to be shipped across the Atlantic from France. In 1726, they tried again to settle their colony. De Pensens, an officer at Louisbourg, was sent to Ile St Jean with a detachment of 25 or 30 men to reorganise the colony and bring out new settlers.

When de Pensens arrived in the spring of 1726, he found the settlements left by St Pierre in ruin. Those who had not returned to Louisbourg clung to life, supplementing their meagre food supply of wheat gleaned from their small plots of land with the fish they were able to catch.

Population	1728	1730
	424	456

The increase in population was accounted for by the few hardy Acadien families who came each year.

The French would not give up on feudalism. They sent a succession of mercantilists and military officers who did little to develop or settle the Island. In 1731, the most serious effort to establish and maintain a settlement was made when La Companie de l'est, under its director Pierre Roma, was granted all the land drained by la Rivière aux Esturgeons (Sturgeon), la Rivière de l'ascension (Brudenell) and la Rivière Achée (Cardigan).

In France the feudal system was crumbling and serfs were being forced off the land to become beggars. Many were jailed for taking food. Roma's first settlers were from among these people. Roma himself arrived in 1732 and immediately set out to fulfil the conditions of the grant and make a profit for his company. However, Roma's enthusiasm was not matched by his partners in France. In 1737 he became sole proprietor of the settlement, under feudal tutelage to Louisbourg.

Although the settlement was never very prosperous, the band of hardy inhabitants built roads from the main port, Trois Rivières to Havre St Pierre, Havre a la Souris, Rivière Achée and Rivière aux Esturgeons.

Population P.E.I.	1735	1748
	563	735

Expulsion and Conquest

Throughout Europe the expansion of trade and the uprisings of the serfs greatly weakened the feudal system. More and more European kings came under the influence and control of the merchants who, as they accumulated greater wealth, became more powerful.

In 1740, Frederick the Great, King of Prussia, allied with England against France and Austria in the War of Austrian Succession. In this new struggle for territorial expansion, the French and English colonies once again became battlegrounds. At this time the population of New England had reached 1,250,-000 and the merchants of New York and Boston were keen to expand their influence and trade.

In 1745, following a 46-day siege, the New Englanders captured the supposedly invincible Louisbourg. At the time of the fall, it was a centre of trade, both legal and illegal. It abounded in gambling houses and brothels. When the New Englanders attacked, the fortress was unprepared. Following their success at Louisbourg, the New Englanders attacked Trois Rivieres and Port La Joye on Ile St Jean, putting those settlements to the torch. Pierre Roma and the Trois Rivières residents, who had nothing to do with the war but who had worked for 13 years to build a prospering enterprise, were ruined and forced to flee before the plundering armies.

The Treaty of Aix-la-Chapelle, ending the War of Austrian Succession in 1748, returned Louisbourg and Ile St Jean to France. The New Englanders never forgave the British for this betrayal. The inhabitants of Ile Royale and Ile St Jean, fishermen, farmers and tradesmen, once again became the unhappy subjects of France.

The Acadiens

For over a decade the Acadiens had been left in peace on the shores of the Bay of Fundy. They "usually lived as members of households which contained three or four generations. Not only was infant mortality extremely low; Acadians lived long and septuagenarians were common. The economic structure of the Acadians meant for the women a preoccupation with weaving, dyeing, knitting and sewing, to produce clothes; with preserving and cooking, with gardening, and with the day-to-day surveillance of the very young and the very old. For the men it meant farming and fishing, hunting and building, tool-making and carpentry in order to produce basic foods, shelter and furniture."[2]

But they were not to be left alone. The English decided to take control of their land. In 1749, the English built the citadel of Halifax as a base against both Louisbourg and Acadie. Again they tried to force the Acadiens to sign the Oath of Allegiance.

The French responded by urging the Acadiens to take up arms against the English, by sending the Micmac on raiding parties against Halifax and by sending French priests among the Acadiens to threaten them with excommunication if they failed to support the French king, Louis XI, "the chosen one of God".

The Acadiens rejected the bribes and threats of the French just as they had rejected the English and they continued to fight for the preservation of their nation. From Beaubassin, Tatamagouche, Baie Verte, Chebouctou, Minus, Cap de Sable and Annapolis Royal they sailed with their cargoes of chickens and pigs, flour and cod, eels and hay, a variety of furs and other goods to sell or trade with both the French and the English; a "crime" for which they were labelled enemies by both sides. Ironically Governor Lawrence in Halifax had no such harsh words for English merchants who openly traded with the French merchants at Louisbourg.

By 1750 approximately 14,000 Acadiens lived along the Bay of Fundy, on the marshes of Chignecto and along the north coast of Nova Scotia. In the next five years almost 2,000 left their homes for Ile St Jean determined to join their kinsmen in preserving their society and building new homes on the ashes left by the New England raiders.

Population	1752	1755
	2,223	2,969

The English were alarmed by this migration to French territory: it strengthened the French. In 1755 the English decided to destroy the Acadien nation. The Acadiens were to be deported; dumped in the English colonies from Boston to the Carolinas. The plan was conceived by the British colonial office, Governor Lawrence of Nova Scotia and some New England merchants.

In early 1755 Charles Morris, a surveyor from Boston, presented Governor Lawrence a detailed report describing how the deportation might be carried out. It said in part:

> The number of men necessary for the deportation of the Acadiens and the choice of places to take them to depends to a large extent on their state of mind. What would greatly encourage them to leave, would be to start the rumour among them that they will all be transported to Canada and to spread this idea on all sides; for it is natural to think that they will scarcely be glad to abandon their goods and offer

Isle St Jean: French map showing settlements (circa 1750). The roads shown here were little more than blazed trails through the forest with logs thrown in swampy areas to keep wagons from bogging down. (PA-PEI).

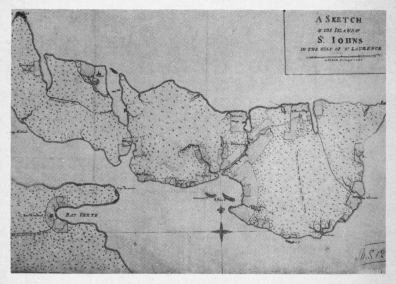

St John Island: English map of 1764 showing where the Acadiens had cleared the land, lived and farmed prior to the expulsion in 1758. (PAC).

themselves to be sent away without knowing where. I believe
that such a persuasion would greatly facilitate the enterprise . . .

If strong detachments are placed in the villages of Minus,
Pizequid and Rivière aux Canards one could, on a particular day, call together all the inhabitants and secure all those
who were present, or perhaps, on a certain Sunday, one
could surround their churches and secure all those who
came, or perhaps in the night enter the villages and take
them abed; . . .[3]

Governor Lawrence then passed on his instructions to Col.
Monckton:

. . . it will be necessary to keep this measure as secret as
possible, as well as to prevent their attempting to escape, as
to carry off their cattle etc., and the better to effect this you
will endeavour to fall upon some stratagem to get the men
both young and old (especially the heads of the families) into
your power and detain them until transportation shall arrive
so as that they may be ready to be shipped off . . .[4]

The day chosen for the deportation was September 5, 1755. The
English attacked three communities in the Annapolis Basin and a
community at Chignecto. The stratagem used by Monckton was
to call the men to a meeting in the community church where they
were held under armed guard. The women and children were then
told to go to their men to wait until the ships, rented from Halifax
and New England merchants, arrived to transport them.

In one of the Annapolis communities the people had a chance
to prepare a resistance. They held the Engish off until some supplies and personal belongings could be gathered up. Then they
escaped to the woods. In all, more than 8,000 made their escape
to Ile St Jean, Ile Royale and New Brunswick.

Despite their superior military might, their lies and deceit, the
English were able to secure fewer than 6,000 Acadiens. After
these besieged people were dispersed, their homes were put to the
torch and their cattle and grain sold to pay the cost of their
expulsion.

The Acadiens refused to be assimilated into the English colonies. Thousands sailed to France only to return to settle in Louisiana, then a French colony. To them France was a foreign country. Some Acadiens who went to France later settled on Belle Isle,

a small island off the south coast of Brittany in north west France. They were to be joined later by other Acadiens after the second expulsion from Ile St Jean in 1758.

In 1756, supplies from Québec helped the Acadiens who escaped to Ile St Jean through their first winter. In the spring they set out tenaciously to farm any available marshland, clear new land and re-establish their communities. The largest settlements were on La Rivière du Nord-Est (Hillsborough), Le Marais (Pownal), Havre St Pierre, Tracadie and Malpeque Bay. They avoided Trois Rivières which was still officially under feudal contract to Pierre Roma.

The land that the Acadiens farmed was granted to them by the commandant, Rousseau de Villejouin. However, many were to lose their land because they lacked the money and the materials to make the improvements demanded by the terms of the grant. Surplus produce, of which there was little, was loaded into ships built by the Acadiens and sent to Louisbourg. Not only did the labour of the farmers help the French but it is reported that young men embittered by the expulsion were taking an active part against the English.

> Sixty of them had been armed and sent over to Acadia in the winter of 1766. They picked up a number of horses and 40 oxen near Pisquid (at Minus Basin). Here also they killed 13 Englishmen, wounded four, and captured a magazine with 300 hogsheads of wheat, 60 of flour, some lard and butter. They also burned two graneries of wheat, a bakery and a mill. In addition to this they aided some Acadians who were in hiding between Cobequid and Tatamagouche to migrate to Isle Saint Jean and carried 500 oxen to Louisbourg.[5]

They also carried out raids against Halifax and in the early spring of 1757 de Villejouin directed the capture of two boats from the English.

Life on Ile St Jean

All these exploits were little help to the hungry refugees on the Island. De Villejouin wrote to his superiors to say that "the women and children dare not go out being unable to hide their nakedness. . . . It is the same for a number of men."[6] The following ex-

<u>Acadien Cabin:</u> *A typical Acadien cabin made out of logs with a thatched roof. Most of the early settlers lived in similar cabins.* (*PAPEI*).

tracts from a census report gives us some idea of what the people endured while rebuilding their nation.

> Paul Boudrot, plowman, native of l'Acadie, aged 49 years, has been two years in the colony. Married to Marie Joseph Duaron, native of l'Acadie, aged 40 years.
>
> They have two sons and three daughters.
>
> Charles Duaron, their father, native of l'Acadie, aged 90 years and infirm. Married to Françoise Godet, native of l'Acadie, aged 85 years.
>
> They have in livestock five oxen, four cows, one sow and four pigs ... They have sown seven bushels of wheat and eight bushels of oats.

> Jean Fraiquingout, ploughman, native of Plauanne, bishopric of Saint Malo, aged 37 years, he has been in the country for two years. Married to Anne Lejeune, native of l'Acadie, aged 35 years.
>
> They have one son and two daughters.
>
> In livestock they have one pig, having lost all besides during the past winter.

> Marie Boudrot, widow of Pierre Richard, very poor, native of l'Acadie, aged 36 years, has been in the country two years.
>
> She has six children, five sons and one daughter.
>
> They have no livestock.
>
> The land on which she is settled is situated on the north bank of the said Riviere du Nord-Est. It was given to her verbally by M. Bonaventure (governor) and he resumes possession as they made no improvements.[7]

In spite of the conditions, the Acadiens spread out over the

Island from Bedecque (Bedeque) to Pointe Rouge (East Point). In only two years they cleared several thousand acres, built grain and saw mills, churches and farm buildings. By 1758 they had established a vigorous if desperately poor society.

Population 1758   4,500
(before the conquest)

The Conquest

The final round in the battle for supremacy between England and France in North America began in 1756. England, again allied with Prussia, went to war with France. Louis XV, the king of France, thought the sugar islands of the French Antilles more valuable than the colonies of North America. His half-hearted effort to defend the North American colonies was no match for British sea power. In 1758, Ile Royale and Ile St Jean were taken. The following year Québec fell.

The English decided to rid themselves of the Acadiens once and for all. In October and November of 1758, ten ships anchored in Port La Joye harbour and soldiers were dispatched to the various settlements to round up the Acadiens. Over 2,000 were seized, loaded on the ships and transported to Europe.

Before they were loaded, most of the single men and women were married on the spot so that the young men would not be immediately conscripted into the army if they landed in France.

Rousseau de Villejouin, in a letter to his superior in France, pleaded the case of the people to no avail.

> It is three years since the last refugees arrived on the island. They had to endure heavy losses and much hardship in getting here, and on arrival, they found themselves so as to speak desperate. Want of provisions and clothing were their companions on the island. I had very little to contribute . . . On their return to France, my Lord, unless you interest yourself in their sufferings and losses, I see them plunged into the most frightful misery that they have ever experienced, such as I can scarcely paint for you. These people will be without food and clothing, unable to procure lodgings and firewood, and knowing not whither to turn in their hour of need. [8]

The letter also explained that the Acadiens sent representatives to the English asking to be allowed to remain on their farms. The English refused. They were still at war with France and the continued existence of the Acadiens on the Island posed a threat.

Many of those who started for Europe perished in the cold waters of the North Atlantic. Three ships that sailed from Port La Joye were lost at sea and 700 drowned. As one ship, the Duke William, foundered in the stormy sea, the priest on board gave the 300 Acadien passengers the last rites. Having performed his priestly duties and consigned the souls of the Acadiens to God, he saved his own skin by jumping into a life boat with the English captain and crew and sailed safely off to England.

Most of the Acadiens who survived the voyage languished in English jails to await the end of the war in 1763. After the Treaty of Paris was signed, over 1,000 Acadiens were released and taken to Belle Isle to join those of their nation who had gone there a few years earlier. Others, dumped unwelcome and unwanted in sea ports along the French coast, became beggars and petty criminals.

Over 1,500 Acadiens living on the north shore and in the interior of Ile St Jean successfully defied deportation by escaping in their fishing boats to Québec, Miramachi, and St Pierre and Miquelon. At Malpeque Bay about 300 took to the woods with their Micmac friends until the deportation was over.

Once again these few remaining returned to their land to re-establish their communities. The 22,000 Acadiens living on the Island today are almost all descendants of these 300 people. In spite of nearly 200 years of discrimination and exploitation, the Acadien people have maintained the culture, language and traditions of their forefathers. Today the descendants of the Acadien nation live in such far flung places as Canada's Maritime provinces, Louisiana in the United States, St Pierre and Miquelon and Belle Isle.

Except for St Pierre and Miquelon off the coast of Newfoundland, which were left to the French as fish stations, the Treaty of Paris turned all the French territories in what is today Canada over to the English.

Chapter Notes

1. Leslie F. Hannon, *Forts of Canada: The Conflicts, Sieges and Battles that Forged a Great Nation*. Toronto, McClelland and Stewart, 1969, p. 30.
2. Naomi Griffiths, *The Acadians: Creation of a People*. Toronto, McGraw-Hill Ryerson, 1973, p. 33.
3. N.E.S. Griffiths, *The Acadian Deportation: Deliberate Perfidy or Cruel Necessity?* Toronto, Copp Clark, 1969, p. 134.
4. Griffiths, *The Acadians* . . . , p. 56.
5. D.C. Harvey, *The French Regime in Prince Edward Island*, pp 184-85.
6. *Ibid.*, p. 186.
7. *Ibid,* pp. 164-65.
8. *Ibid.*, pp 192-93.

4

Establishing
British control

British North America

After the conquest, imperial Britain controlled a huge empire in
North America: a) the Thirteen Colonies along the Atlantic Coast,
b) the former colonies of France along the St Lawrence River, and
c) the maritime colonies along the Gulf of St Lawrence.

In the Thirteen Colonies a strong merchant class challenged
British mercantilists by building up a lucrative trade in rum, furs
and wheat with both British and French colonies in the West
Indies. The British merchants levied new taxes and duties on their
imports. The Thirteen Colonies refused to pay.

Seeing more trouble ahead, the British moved to strengthen
their control over the newly conquered people of New France. Because there were more than one hundred thousand of them, the
solution was not to be found in mass expulsion as had been done
with the Acadiens. Other means of control had to be adopted.
And they were at hand. Being so addicted themselves to power
and privilege, the British imperialists turned with unerring
shrewdness to like-minded addicts—the Church of Rome and the
Seigneurs. The Church was permitted to continue collecting
tithes, the Bishops allowed to enjoy the power they had wielded
under the French and the Seigneurs, with their rights and lands
intact, paid untroublesome tribute to the new masters at Québec
City. And if feudalism paid off with Britain's former enemies in

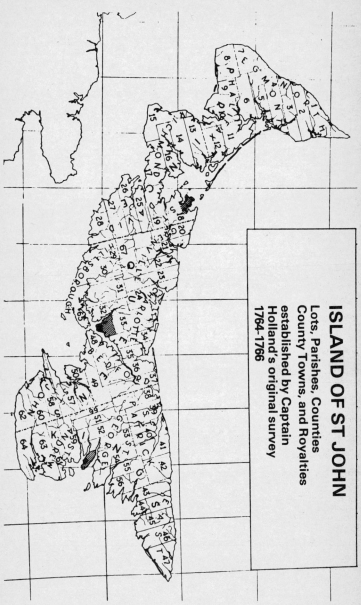

ISLAND OF ST JOHN
Lots, Parishes, Counties
County Towns, and Royalties
established by Captain
Holland's original survey
1764-1766

<u>Lot and Parish Map:</u> *The lots and parishes as drawn up by Captain Samuel Holland in his survey 1765-1766. (PAPEI).*

New France, why not in the new colony of St John's Island?

The Land Lottery

Members of the British aristocracy, not content with their vast land holdings in the British Isles, soon turned their greedy eyes towards the new colony.

The Earl of Egmont, in 1763, petitioned George III, called George The Mad, for a grant of the whole island, to be set up as a feudal domain with himself as overlord. The Island was to be divided into *hundreds* of 40,000 acres each, the hundreds to be subdivided into *manors* of 2,000 acres each. These in turn were to be divided into *freeholds* of 200 acres each. Each hundred was to be ruled by a capital lord who was to have a *desesme* (private estate) of 10,000 acres. Each hundred was to have a town and each of the manor lords and freeholders was to have a town lot and residence according to his position in the hierarchy of the feudal pyramid. The freeholder was to do all the productive work and account for all the rent. The Earl of Egmont was to pay none.

The Colonial Office decided that the Island was too small for Egmont's scheme and his petition was denied. He was advised to ask for Cape Breton instead but he turned it down. A number of similar petitions were presented to the Colonial Office. While all were turned down, it was upon this model that the Island was finally divided.

In 1765, the Island was surveyed by Samuel Holland. It was divided into three counties: Kings in the east with its county town, Georgetown (after George III); Queen's in the centre with its county town, Charlottetown (after the king's wife, Charlotte); and Prince in the west with its country town, Princetown. Surrounding each town an area of over 6000 acres called a *royalty* was reserved as pasture lots for town residents. (These areas are still called royalties today.) The remainder of the Island was divided into 67 lots of approximately 20,000 acres each.

In 1767, lots 40 and 59 were granted to persons who had already established fishing operations along their shores. Lot 66 was reserved for the crown. The imperial government then invited military officers, petty nobility and prominent merchants to petition for grants of the remaining 64 lots. The petition of John Condon illustrates the basis on which retired military men sought favor from the crown.

> Your petitioner has served in the war of 1769 and all the late wars in America, has been six times wounded, three of which wounds were at the siege of Quebec, and has two balls lodged, one in the hand and one in the joint of the shoulder...[1]

But foot soldiers like Condon received no grants.

The petitioners were interviewed by the Colonial Office in London and 64 were selected to participate in a lottery. On July 23, 1767, the 64 names were put in a box and the lots assigned in order as they were drawn.

The grants were to be given on the following conditions:

Each of the lots was to be settled by one person per hundred acres within ten years.

This would mean 200 persons per lot on the average. There were no regulations as to how the land was to be held by the new settlers. This was left entirely to the discretion of the landlords. In fact most landlords required settlers to lease the land and pay a yearly rent. A few grantees sold their assigned lots immediately but most retained ownership for speculative purposes. By leasing their land they saw its value increasing yearly through the efforts of their tenants who cleared and cultivated. These landlords expended not one ounce of labour yet they, their families and successors, right down to the present day, fattened and prospered through the labours of their toiling tenants.

The land was to be settled by foreign protestants from the Thirteen Colonies and other European countries.

Industrial expansion in Britain had created a labour shortage so the English could not afford to send people to the colonies. Secondly, since the English were trying to suppress the Catholic religion they would not encourage Catholics to inhabit this new colony. Furthermore, faced with rebellion in the Thirteen Colonies, they wanted the dissatisfied there to move so that they would be in a stronger position to keep the rest of the people in line.

Each landlord was to pay an annual rent, called a quit rent, to the Colonial Office in London.

Quit rents were set at 2, 4, or 6 shillings per hundred acres according to Holland's assessment of the value of the land. The landlords usually charged their tenants one shilling per acre the first year. This was increased as the tenants cleared the land and increased its value. Even at 1s per acre, a fully settled lot stood to yield huge profits for its owner. Each lot was to reserve 100 acres for the Church of England, 30 acres for the schoolmaster and a 500 foot frontage on all land bordering on water for the fisheries.

Failure to comply with these conditions was to mean forfeiture of the land to the crown. But as we shall soon see, they were not taken seriously by either the landlords or the Colonial Office.

The Island was at first made a part of Nova Scotia under the colonial administration at Halifax. In 1769, the resident landlords requested a separate government. They argued that poor communications especially during winter when the Strait was ice-bound made it impossible to govern the Island from Halifax. They proposed that the quit rents be used to pay the cost of local government so there would be no additional expense to Britain. The Colonial Office agreed and, that same year, Walter Patterson was sent as the first governor.

The Acadiens

For the first few years after the conquest the Island's non-native population was almost entirely made up of the remaining Acadiens. Once again they were working energetically to rebuild their society on the ruins left after the conquest. The first new immigrants were adventurers from New England and Britain. They set up communities in Malpeque, Rustico, Tracadie, and St Peter's where they employed Acadiens in the fisheries.

Population 1758 (after conquest)

Acadiens	about 300
Other white	64

The Acadien population may have been larger than the official figures state. Pockets of self-sufficient settlers, such as the one visited by Lt. Governor Fanning at Bay Fortune in 1770, remained unknown to the British for a number of years.

Life in these small communities was hard. Completely isolated from each other in winter, the people had to rely on scanty food supplies of water, potatoes and salt fish. The little grain they grew was bartered for necessities such as salt with British ships passing on their way to and from the West Indies.

New Settlement

While the majority of landlords did nothing to encourage settlement, there were a few exceptions. The first of the land speculators to encourage settlement was James Montgomery who, by 1775, had acquired 65,000 acres of land, lots 30 and 34, 1/2 of lot 12 and 2/3 of lot 54, in addition to the 20,000 acre lot 7 bestowed upon him by the lottery of 1767.

In May 1770, Montgomery persuaded a number of tenant farmers, about 200 in all, from Perthshire, Scotland that they would have a much better life on his lands on Lot 34 at Covehead and pay a lower rent. The 1s per acre seemed reasonable to the prospective settlers until they arrived to find the land covered with forest.

Montgomery himself remained in England and contributed little to get the settlement going. Many of the new arrivals were forced because of lack of provisions to go to Pictou in Nova Scotia to live with kinsmen who had already settled there.

Another settlement was started in 1770 by Robert Stewart, who with his family and about 200 settlers from Argyleshire, Scotland, arrived on lot 18 at Malpeque, near Princeton. Their ship, the *Annabella*, ran aground in Princeton harbour and, although no lives were lost, most of their provisions were, and they suffered severely that first winter.

In the autumn of 1771, the Malpeque settlers were joined by about seventy new arrivals who came without assistance from any landlord.

Smaller settlements were established around 1770-71 by Captain Holland on lot 28 at Tryon, James Richardson, near Charlottetown, Lt. Governor DesBrisay on lot 31 and 32 west of

Battle of Culloden Moor

The Battle of Culloden Moor, 1745, led by "Bonnie Prince Charlie" marked the end of the Scottish uprising, the last major strike for Scottish independence against British rule. Since 1707, the highlanders had been fighting the English. Although divided by religion and clan rivalries, they were united as a man in their hatred of English oppression.

In a number of battles the fierce highland fighters had cut the English army to ribbons. At Culloden, the English massed a well-armed, well-provisioned army which outnumbered the highlanders two-to-one. The Scottish attack on the English army was unparalleled in the history of courageous deeds. They were overpowered. 1,200 highlanders were slaughtered on the moors when the English commander ordered the wounded butchered where they lay.

The survivors of the battle escaped into the highlands where they were hunted like animals.

The English imperialists had to secure "their own" island before they could safely set out to conquer the world. That meant crushing the distinct Scottish nation that lived on their northern borders. The viciousness with which they carried this out is indicated by the sentence passed on the Scottish prisoners:

You and every one of you, prisoners at the bar, return to the prison from whence you came, and from there you must be drawn to the place of execution; when you come there you must be hanged by the neck not till you be dead, for you must be cut down alive—then your bowels must be taken out and burnt before your faces; then your heads must be severed from your bodies, and your bodies divided each into four quarters, and they must be at the king's disposal, and God have mercy on your

> soul.[2]
> Only one in twenty of the prisoners was
> brought to trial, the rest were transported to be
> indentured servants or sold as slaves.
> But the Scottish spirit was not broken. They
> continued to fight against British oppression. As
> the enclosures took more and more of their land
> for pasture, they were driven deeper and deeper
> into the highlands and land holdings became
> smaller and smaller. Faced with the continued
> threat of English raids and famine, immigration
> became a necessity.

Charlottetown in the West River area and by Robert Clark on lot
21 at New London. Clark was a Quaker and this settlement was
set up originally as a Quaker colony for members of that denomi-
nation who were being persecuted by the Church of England.
Although it did not continue as a Quaker colony, New London
has survived until the present day.

The largest of the new settlements was established by Captain
John MacDonald. In 1771, with funds provided by the Roman
Catholic Church, MacDonald brought 300 Scottish highlanders
to his land on lot 36 at Tracadie. The highlanders were victims of
persecution by their Presbyterian landlord in northern Scotland
where they and many hundreds of others had been driven after
their defeat by the "Bloody English Butcher", the Duke of
Cumberland.

Arriving on the Island, these Scottish settlers had to carve
homesteads out of the forest. One of the settlers, Alex Shaw, who
settled at West River, left this description of the labour that went
into building a new settlement:

> After having cut a small piece out of the forest as close to
> the river as possible, a house is erected mostly of round logs
> dovetailed at the corners, the chinks between the logs being
> tightly caulked with moss; the roof is covered with bark
> taken from fur or spruce trees, or else sedge grass from the
> marshes. The floor is the ground, smoothly packed, and a
> huge fireplace in the centre of the floor, with a hole in the

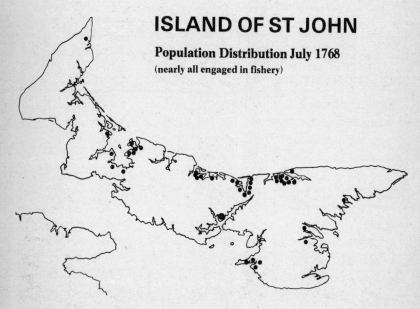

ISLAND OF ST JOHN

Population Distribution July 1768
(nearly all engaged in fishery)

Settlement 1768: *Map showing the scattered settlement ten years after the expulsion of the Acadiens.*

roof for the exit of smoke.[3]

After the house was built there was no rest for the settlers as they struggled to clear more land and expand their homesteads:

Clearing the land is a slow and hard process. First the trees are cut and their branches are cut off. Their trunks are cut in lengths of 12 to 14 feet. This operation is called junking. When the space intended to be cleared is cut down, junked with logs and branches lying around all over the clearing, fire is applied to it on as dry and windy a day as can be selected. If this fire burns well the greatest part of the small branches are consumed, but the trunks are only scorched. The trunks are then rolled together and made into piles.

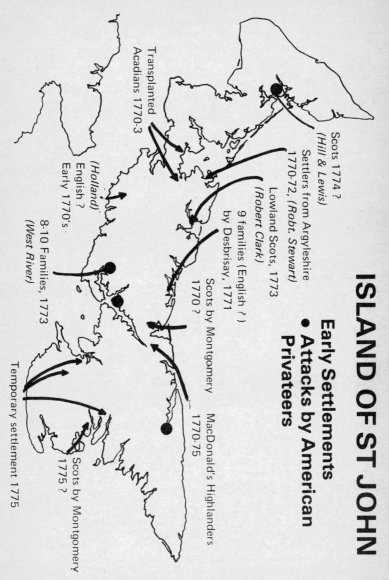

ISLAND OF ST JOHN

Early Settlements
• Attacks by American Privateers

Scots 1774 ?
(Hill & Lewis)

Settlers from Argyleshire
1770-72, (Robt. Stewart)

Transplanted
Acadians 1770-3

(Holland)
English ?
Early 1770's

8-10 Families, 1773
(West River)

Lowland Scots, 1773
(Robert Clark)

9 families (English ?)
by Desbrisay, 1771

Scots by Montgomery
1770 ?

MacDonald's Highlanders
1770-75

Temporary settlement 1775

Scots by Montgomery
1775 ?

Early English Settlement: *Map showing where the early English settlement grew up. Also shown are the settlements attacked by American privateers during the American Revolution. A large number of the Acadiens
had moved from Malpeque to an area just west of the present day
Summerside by 1773.*

The remaining branches are gathered up and thrown upon the heavier wood to help it burn. This operation is often repeated three or four times before the wood is all burned.

After the wood is all burned the stumps are left standing about two feet high. The settlers then plant their potatoes in mounds resembling ant hills among the stumps. The ash is used as fertilizer. The whole family participates. In this way the settlers clear a small piece of land each year, adding to the area they can plant. After a number of years the stumps rot away until they can be removed.[4]

Life was hard, even in the best of times. But there were other hazards as well.

In 1774, many of the settlements were attacked by field mice so ferocious that they ate the potatoes right out of the ground. This plague destroyed most of the crops. The town of Souris (French for mouse) on the north east coast of the Island stands as a memorial to the plague. In 1775, the new settlement at West River was raided by American privateers who robbed the settlers of their winter provisions.

Severe hardship confronted a new settlement when winter provisions were not to be had:

That winter they would have perished were it not for a French settlement some miles distant from which they received supplies, principally potatoes, in exchange for the clothing they had brought with them from Scotland, until they scarcely retained sufficient to clothe themselves decently. From a shortage of food the men became reduced to such a state of weakness, and the snow was so deep, that they became at last scarcely able to carry back provisions for their families, and when with slow steps and heavy labour, they brought them home such was the state of weakness in which they left their children, they trembled to enter their dwellings lest they should find them dead, and sometimes waited at the door, listening for any sound that might indicate that they were alive.[5]

While the heroic settlers fought starvation in wretched conditions, the government officials in Charlottetown were upset because their salaries had not been paid. The landlords in England had not paid their quit rents.

Population 1775   1215

Chapter Notes

1. Public Archives of Canada (PAC), M.G. 11, C.O. 217, p. 130.
2. David Johnstone Beatty, "Prince Charles and the Border Land", in Greg Keilty (ed.), *1837: Revolution in the Canadas*, Toronto, NC Press, 1974, pp. 16-17.
3. Walter Johnstone, "A Series of Letters, Descriptions of Prince Edward Island in the Gulf of St. Lawrence" in D.C. Harvey (ed.) *Journeys to the Island of Saint John*, Toronto, Mac-Millan, 1955, pp. 107-108.
4. *Ibid.*, pp. 107-108.
5. D.C. Harvey, "Early Settlement and Social Conditions in Prince Edward Island" in *Dalhousie Review*, January 1932, p. 457.

5

The American Revolution: pillagers and profiteers

Raids on the Island

The merchants in the Thirteen Colonies finally felt that they were strong enough to rid themselves of English taxes and interference in their trade with the West Indies. In 1774, the American Revolution began. Canada was attacked as the revolutionaries attempted to capture the large supply of British arms in Québec City and rid themselves of the threat of loyal British colonies on their northern borders.

In Québec, the clergy and the seigneurs remained firm allies of the English. When the revolutionaries attacked in 1775, many *habitants* were tempted to join the Americans but they lacked organisation and leadership. The Americans captured Montréal and Trois Rivières but were stopped at the citadel of Québec. Those habitants who considered joining the Americans soon realized that the "freedom" they were offered was in reality only the freedom to become subjects of the new American republic. They feared that they would be just as much dominated under the Americans as under the English. Liberation for the Québec people could only come from the Québec people themselves.

The lack of solid support from the people of Québec and the superior sea power of the British (which brought new supplies and arms) brought about the collapse of the U.S. invasion of Canada. British sea power also prevented the revolutionaries from launching a concerted attack on the Maritime colonies or from lending effective support to sympathisers of the revolution.

On the Island, a few British settlers were recruited to defend Québec in 1775. The Acadiens however were openly sympathetic to the revolution. Acting governor Phillips Callbeck said that the Acadiens "almost to a man are disaffected and . . . publically express their wishes that the rebels may come. The Indians (Micmac) also oppose the British but are held down because, although they are well armed, they have little ammunition." [1]

While sympathy for the revolutionaries was widespread among the people of the Maritimes, their dispersed settlements lacked the cohesion, economic and social development necessary to join.

Totally undefended except for a poorly armed 100-man militia, the Island was easy prey for U.S. adventurers. The war had cut off British consumer goods. Privateers stepped in, supplying goods to needy settlers at greatly inflated prices.

On November 27, 1775, U.S. troops in fishing schooners sent to harass British ships in the Gulf of St. Lawrence attacked and pillaged Charlottetown. Phillips Callbeck and Surveyor-General George Wright were captured and taken to Cambridge, Mass. Callbeck's house was burned and the colony's meagre provisions were plundered. Later in 1775, American privateers pillaged a settlement in lot 5, stealing the provisions of the 103 settlers. The West River settlement was also attacked that same year.

These were not planned military attacks, but raids against the undefended British outposts. The people suffered greatly, but the attacks were of no strategic significance.

Callbeck and Wright were released by General George Washington on May 1, 1776. Washington opposed the raids because he realised that they turned the people of the other colonies against the revolutionary forces.

Upon his return Callbeck begged the British Colonial Office to send help. The Colonial Office told him to raise a militia from among the people. But what use was a militia without guns and ammunition?

Despite Washington's opposition, the attacks continued. In 1778, St. Peter's was attacked by two fishing schooners and all the provisions were stolen. Life for the 1200 settlers was difficult enough! Like the Quebécois, they soon turned against all ideas of joining the new American republic.

The Americans, assisted by the French who were anxious to redeem their losses in the Seven Years War, declard their independence on July 4, 1776.

The revolutionary war ended in victory in 1783.

The revolution in the United States was part of the world bourgeois-democratic revolution against feudalism and mercantile capitalism and the first major strike against colonialism. It unleashed new forces of capitalism which greatly expanded production.

The United Empire Loyalists

After the revolution, many of those in the former thirteen colonies who had sided with the British, departed from the new republic. Of the one hundred thousand "loyalists" who left, forty thousand went to the British maritime colonies. Some were the victims of the circumstances of war but many others left resolved to continue their lives of privilege under the British crown. These latter were, of course, among the most reactionary inhabitants of the former thirteen colonies.

In 1784, Governor Patterson decided to kill two birds with one stone. He wanted new settlers for St John Island and he wanted to strengthen his own hand in his dispute with the Colonial Office over the lands he had sold for non-payment of rent.

Patterson sent government representatives to Shelbourne, Nova Scotia where a large number of loyalists had camped. His agents were to lure them to the Island with offers of land and free passage.

The new settlers endured great hardship in their first winter on the Island. When they arrived in August with nothing but the clothes on their backs, too late to raise a crop, they were housed in the barracks in Charlottetown and survived on rations distributed from the military's inadequate stores.

As soon as spring arrived, a number returned to Nova Scotia where they hoped to find better conditions. Patterson settled

<u>Walter Patterson:</u> *The first governor of St John Island, 1769-1784 and first Lt-Governor 1784-1786* (*PAPEI*).

those who remained on land claimed for non-payment of rent and a few were given deeds. Some of the wealthy Loyalists brought their slaves to Summerside, Princeton and Charlottetown. For a few years they worked for their owners and later became "free". Most moved to Nova Scotia where a number of black people had settled.

The Struggle for Land

The island colony's government was in the hands of the Governor, appointed by the British crown, and a Council appointed by the British government in London on the advice of the Governor. The Assembly, although nominally a part of the government, in fact was a mere debating chamber in which the wind of public opinion might be tested. All legislation to do with property and the constitution required the approval of the government in London. Before long, disagreements arose between Charlottetown and the Colonial Office.

In 1774 the Island government passed a law giving it power to sell, by public auction, land on which quit rents had not been paid. The proceeds from the sale were to go to the government. This act got the assent of the Colonial Office. Only government officials were notified of the time of the auction and the successful bidders took the land in lieu of salaries owing them.

The absentee landlords in London were furious. They lobbied to convince the Colonial Office to prevent the Island government from selling their land. When, in 1781, further legislation was passed by Patterson to cover land excluded from the 1774 Act, the Colonial Office refused assent.

Gov. Patterson wanted to turn over the land to resident Islanders like himself so that the commerce of the colony would not be in the hands of absentee landlords in London. However, the effects of the war with the Thirteen Colonies plus the influence of the absentee landlords convinced London that putting this kind of power into the hands of the colony's government was not in the interest of British imperialism. Patterson was stopped from carrying out his intention.

An order was sent out to repeal the 1774 legislation and to

return the land to its former owners. Patterson refused to obey.

The following year the Colonial Office sent an already prepared bill which would rescind the two former acts. Patterson was instructed to place it before the Assembly. Again he refused.

The unity of the resident landlords was broken when Patterson and Chief Justice Stewart quarrelled over part of the land sold in 1774 and an affair Patterson was having with Stewart's wife. Stewart saw the opportunity to remain in the good graces of the Colonial Office by turning the quarrel into a political attack on Patterson. He threw in his lot with the absentee landlords and, with other functionaries, became the Colonial Office's resident champion against Patterson.

Patterson continued to fight. He refused to put the bill before the Assembly because the majority, all of whom were residents of Charlottetown, supported Stewart. He called an election, hoping to get a majority that would reject the bill. When the newly elected Assembly was no more sympathetic than the old one, Patterson dissolved it in 1784. In the following election, he issued writs only in those areas where he was sure of success and this time he got the assembly he wanted. An act was promptly passed rendering legal the Act of 1781 and brushing aside the bill from London.

The Colonial Office had had enough. Patterson was recalled.

The man sent to replace him was Edmund Fanning. After the revolutionary war, Fanning had been forced out of North Carolina, where he had been a supreme court judge. He had subsequently served the British as Lt.-Governor of Nova Scotia for four years before coming to the Island. He brought his family and two slaves with him.

When Fanning arrived in November, 1786, Patterson had already received orders to return to London. Patterson however continued to fight, refusing to turn over the government. In April 1787, he again received orders to leave for Britain. This time he complied but only after going to Québec City to consult with the governor-general—from whom he got no support.

The landlords in London were not content with Patterson's dismissal. They charged him and his supporters in the Council with criminal actions and had them dismissed both from Council and

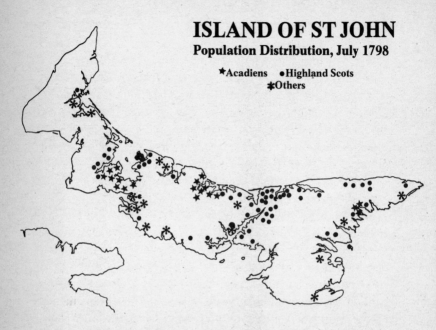

ISLAND OF ST JOHN
Population Distribution, July 1798

★Acadiens ●Highland Scots
✱Others

Population Map: *Distribution of population in 1798. Note the complete absence of population in the western region and in the interior of both King's and Queen's counties.*

from government office.

The absentee landlords and the Colonial Office were successful in defeating the first fight for independence on the Island. But mostly the island landlords were defeated by their own weakness, by lack of organisation and by their undemocratic practices.

Chapter Notes

1. PAC., M.G. 11, C.O. 226, "Callbeck to Germain", May 20, 1776.

6

The Family Compact

The Fanning Régime

The struggle for control of land on the Island forced the British to consolidate their base of power. In 1784, the Island had been returned to the jurisdiction of the governor of Nova Scotia. Patterson had been demoted to lieutenant-governor with his power intact except when the governor was on the Island in person. A few years later the British further consolidated the North American colonies by bringing them all under one governor-general, Sir Guy Carleton, who resided in Québec.

When Fanning took over as lieutenant-governor, he immediately allied himself with Stewart and took steps to crush the Patterson group which represented the majority of the resident landlords. His first act was to dismiss the pro-Patterson Assembly and get a new one elected which supported the Stewart faction.

He further consolidated his position by inviting his English friends to fill the Council seats and other government offices. By 1801, seven of the seventeen government officials, including judges, were members of the Stewart family. Another seven were Fanning's personal appointees!

As long as this comprador* Family Compact kept the land-

---

* The Portuguese word *Comprador* (meaning buyer) was first used for the Chinese manager or senior employee in Portugal's commercial establishments in China and has now come to refer generally to that class of people in a colony who buy status and profit for themselves by helping the imperialist power exploit their fellow colonials.

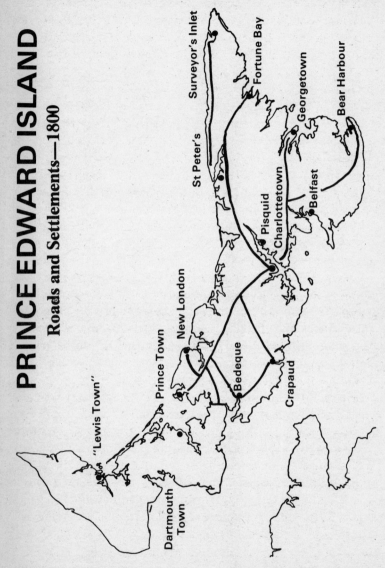

PRINCE EDWARD ISLAND
Roads and Settlements—1800

Surveyor's Inlet

Fortune Bay

Georgetown

Bear Harbour

St Peter's

Pisquid

Charlottetown

Belfast

New London

Prince Town

"Lewis Town"

Bedeque

Crapaud

Dartmouth Town

Roads 1800: *The roads were narrow trails through the woods which allowed wagon traffic and then only in summer. Although not shown, there were road houses or taverns located along the road every 5 to 7 miles where travellers could stop to eat and feed their horses or stay overnight.*

lords in London happy, they were given free rein to rule the colony as their private domain. The Compact did everything possible to cater to the absentee landlords and missed no opportunity to attack the opposition. They could inflict any oppression on the people that they wished.

Nevertheless the resident landlords continued to fight. Captain John MacDonald found that copies of certain acts and land titles filed in Charlottetown were different from the copies sent to the Colonial Office in London. The Compact didn't dare let the Colonial Office know what skullduggery they were up to. The Colonial Office didn't know and didn't ask, as long as the London landlords were contented. When MacDonald threatened to reveal what he knew, Fanning attempted to bribe him by offering him a commission in the militia. MacDonald refused. Fanning promptly fabricated a charge of libel against him and had him thrown in jail.

Another resident landlord, John Hill, owner of five lots in Western Prince County, wrote a long letter to the Colonial Office describing how Fanning falsified documents and agitated the tenantry. Hill and other resident landlords wanted to bring out settlers but the state of unrest, they claimed, discouraged new settlers from coming.

When Hill and MacDonald opposed the Fanning régime, they were dealt with quickly and ruthlessly. In his letter, Hill described how "the sheriff came in the night and attacked the stores of goods and took everything—the people were left to disperse without substance."[1]

During the Fanning régime, most of the quit rents paid in Charlottetown by resident landlords were not recorded. The money went directly into the pockets of Compact members. The Colonial Office, even when informed, closed its eyes to this practice. It was a small price to pay for keeping from public knowledge the fact that non-resident landlords paid no rent at all.

Fanning and the Compact not only pocketed the quit rents due to the crown; they exercised, unlawfully, the right of escheat. (Escheat is a legal term. It means the reverting of property to the crown when there are no legal heirs or when certain conditions

A Settler's Home: *By 1800, the frame boarded-in and shingled house had replaced the thatch roofed cabin for most settlers. (PAPEI).*

pertaining to the land holding are unfulfilled.) Whereas Patterson had been ordered back to London for confiscating the land of influential absentee landlords, Fanning and the Compact gang were confiscating the land of defaulting local landlords.

When the tenants saw the government causing the escheat of land, they thought it was part of a general policy of escheat and that henceforth, the tenants would pay their rents on escheated land directly to the government, their new landlord.

Of course this situation caused great instability. The feudal system of landholding, the domination of absentee landlords, and the carnage perpetrated on local landlords completely stopped the development of merchant trade and wage labour which characterised the emergence of capitalism. In other British colonies, and to an even greater extent in the United States, a bourgeois merchant class had risen to prominence. On the Island, there were only a few merchants, described more accurately, perhaps as "village shopkeepers". During Fanning's despotic régime many were forced to take up farming in order to live.

Because the absentee landlords were not making the profits

they wanted, they petitioned the Colonial Office for a re-adjustment of the quit rents in 1802. The Colonial Office ordered a reduction. Under the new scale landlords were supposed to pay a reduced rate, with higher payment on unsettled lands. Overall the quit rents were cut from a theoretical total of £59,162 to £18,732, in spite of the fact that 40 of the 67 lots were unsettled. The reduced rents were to be paid within a year.

In 1803, the Assembly, composed of a majority sympathetic to the resident landlords and tenants, passed a resolution calling for a Court of Escheat to confiscate *all* lands for which the reduced rent had not been paid. Fanning, the Compact, the absentee landlords and the Colonial Office opposed the resolution. Colonial Secretary Hobart argued that because the landlords had made such great sacrifices in the American Revolutionary War, they were unable to meet their commitments on the Island. These contributions, he said, were responsible for keeping the Island in the "glorious servitude" of Britain, more correctly in the "glorious servitude" of the absentee landlords and Fanning's gang. The American Revolutionary War had been over for twenty years.

During the period dealt with in this chapter (1784-1803), the only change of any significance in the Island's history was a change of name. In 1799, to avoid confusion with the town of St John in New Brunswick and the capital of the colony of Newfoundland (St John's), the Island was re-named Prince Edward Island after King George IV's brother. Thirty-eight years later, Edward's daughter, Victoria, was to become Queen of England.

Chapter Notes

1. PAC, M.G. 11, C.O. 226, "John Hill Memorial", February 11, 1808.

7

Nation building—
invasion repulsed

The Society of Loyal Electors

The landlords continued to pay little of their quit rent, despite its reduction. The tenants, of course, who laboured to clear the land, build the homesteads and raise the crops, received no relief by way of reduced rents. Indeed, all able-bodied farmers and their sons were required to spend several days a year building and maintaining the roads. This practice, called *corvée*, was a feudal obligation; a service to the landlords. It made their land more accessible and thus more valuable.

The absentee landlords managed their affairs through land agents who collected the rents and arranged leases for the tenants. These agents lived in comfort in Charlottetown or on country estates, going to the farms only to collect rents or to confiscate a tenant's property when his rent was not paid. This they did at some risk to life and much risk to limb. They were regarded by the tenants as little more than highwaymen. Not all, perhaps not even half, of the rents were collected.

The tenants' demands for government escheat of land were growing. In 1796, they protested by refusing to serve in the militia. When Fanning dissolved the Assembly after it passed the Escheat Resolution in 1803, the tenants promptly elected members of the *Society of Loyal Electors* to the new Assembly.

The Loyal Electors, who opposed the landlords and advocated escheat, were led by James B. Palmer, a lawyer who came from Dublin, Ireland in 1802 to seek his fortune and by William Hazzard, the son of a loyalist. Most of them were petit-bourgeois* lawyers and merchants from Charlottetown, who wanted an independent economy. Others were rural tenants, including a majority of the loyalists.

The demand for escheat was on a firm legal foundation and indeed had been practiced by both Patterson and Fanning. The landlords had not fulfilled the requirements of their grants and by law the land should have reverted to the crown. However, the landlords' friends in London and Charlottetown were not about to abide by legal statutes which stood in the way of their vested interests.

Branches of the Loyal Electors were set up in different parts of the Island and action was taken to get sympathetic candidates elected to the Assembly. In 1804, the Assembly again passed a motion calling for escheat and again it was rejected by the Compact. The same excuse was made: the patriotic landlords were busy supporting Britain's wars (now the war with Napoleon), and were unable to look after their affairs on the Island.

Population 1804   6,957

Opposition to the Compact continued to grow. Before more trouble occurred, the authorities in London decided to remove Fanning. So low was his esteem that the Colonial Office announced his recall in the press before informing him officially. Fanning read of his recall one spring morning in 1804 when he opened the newspapers from Britain. He had to wait until July for official word of his fate.

His replacement, J. F. W. DesBarres, had spent sixteen years in London trying to disprove charges of disloyalty arising from ear-

---

*In capitalist society the bourgeoisie is the class which owns the means of production and hires wage labourers to do its work. Wage labourers are the proletariat, that class of people which owns no means of production and has no commodity to sell except this labour power. The petit bourgeoisie is the class which bears characteristics of both the primary contending classes.

lier efforts on behalf of himself and the Empire. Now this former lieutenant-governor of Cape Breton Island set out, busily, at the age of 83 to vindicate himself in the eyes of the Colonial Office.

His intial report showed that in forty years of British rule only 4,947 of the 1,369,000 acres had been cleared. Determined to change this, DesBarres attacked the obvious cause of this situation, the Compact. He turned for help to J.B. Palmer. Palmer was appointed to no less than eight offices and, with DesBarres' blessing, effectively took over the administration of the colony. Palmer was appointed also judge of the Chancery Court* whereupon he arranged to have all cases tried in that court.

When, in 1812, Chief Justice Colclaugh of the Supreme Court and an associate of the Compact, opposed the Society of Loyal Electors, the Assembly asked DesBarres to suspend him. DesBarres was quick to comply. Although the Society now held sway over all three levels of the local colonial government, the veto power of the metropolis prevented any progressive legislation from becoming law.

In 1812, DesBarres was removed from office at the request of the deposed Chief Justice, Colclaugh, and the Compact. In a letter to the Colonial Office, Colclaugh said: "Democracy is making such rapid strides here that without [unless] some man of firmness and sense is sent, or the Island is annexed to Nova Scotia, I really trouble for its safety should there be a war with America."[1]

Poor old DesBarres was unsuccessful in his attempt to vindicate himself. He knew that for there to be progress he had to broaden the class representation in the government. But, he and Palmer moved with imprudent haste. They failed to organise the support of the tenants and concentrated all governmental power in the hands of one man. DesBarres retired to Nova Scotia where he lived in disgrace to the age of 104.

The War of 1812-1814

By 1750, the English bourgeoisie was in firm control of the British

---

*Chancery Court was a separate court of equity for cases with no remedy in Common Law. It was an important legal body in P.E.I. because many cases did not come under existing laws.

Isles. The French bourgeoisie overthrew the remnants of feudalism in the French Revolution of 1789. When Napoleon Bonaparte became First Consul of the French Republic, the French bourgeoisie felt ready to expand its influence to the other countries of Europe. By 1805, France controlled most of Europe except the British Isles and Russia. Britain and France blockaded each other's ports.

With the British preoccupied in Europe, the U.S. took the opportunity to expand into the Ohio territory, vacated by the British in 1798. Napoleon, needing money for his European wars, in 1803 sold the Louisiana territory, bought previously from Spain, to the U.S. for fifteen million dollars.

In 1812, acting on the principle "when the cat's away the mice will play" the U.S. attacked British North America once again to liberate it from British rule.

"The militia of Kentucky are alone competent to place Montréal and Upper Canada at our feet" said Henry Clay. "A mere matter of marching"[2] said Jefferson.

As in the American Revolutionary War, there was some interest in the British colonies in being liberated from British rule. But this was turned to active opposition when U.S. troops burned and looted small pioneer settlements along the border. The people of Canada rallied and fought fiercely and well against the invaders. In battles from Windsor to Montréal and in Halifax during two years of fighting the U.S. was unable to gain any territory by force of arms. The Americans had not counted on the determination of the people of the colonies to rally and fight against the invasion. Their arrogance brought them humiliating defeat. But the treaties of 1814 and 1818 signed by the British handed the U.S. much of the Ohio territory, which had been under British control and inhabited by Canada's native allies before the war.

In P.E.I., the Loyal Electors had some sympathy for the U.S. because it was fighting their common enemy—the British. However, as in the Revolutionary War, the petty bourgeoisie was not strong enough or well enough organised to launch its own war of independence.

The Island in 1812

After the DesBarres episode, the British took strong action to stem the growing influence of the Island petty bourgeoisie. The man chosen to do the job was the despotic Charles Douglas Smith, a relative of the Colonial Secretary, Lord Bathurst, and a brother of a British admiral. By allying with the Compact, Smith was soon able to reinstate the landlords to their former position of absolute power. The Island petty bourgeoisie was too weak to consolidate the gains it had made. Palmer was charged with malpractice and the Loyal Electors were forced underground.

One of the leaders of the attack on the Loyal Electors was Thomas Douglas, the fifth Earl of Selkirk who was later to become Canada's largest landlord. In 1803 he purchased a large block of land in the Belfast area of P.E.I. and brought out settlers from Scotland. He also established settlements in Southwestern Ontario and in the Northwest—present-day Manitoba. His tenants were destitute Scottish crofters, the heirs of Culloden, whom he set to cultivating his land and producing crops. He profited from the sale of the crops and the rents levied each year on the tenants.

Selkirk was an enlightened imperialist who realised the importance of settlement—both to the future strength of the British empire and for present profit. And if he was to get the most out of his tenants, he had to give them long leases so that they would feel secure enough to stay to develop the land, work hard and pay the rent. He seldom visited the settlements but left them in the hands of agents.

Despite his liberal sentiments Selkirk was totally opposed to any movement toward independence in the British colonies. He supported the despotic Charles Smith in P.E.I. and similarly the Hudson's Bay Company in Manitoba. By 1814, Selkirk and John Cambridge, another absentee, were the largest landlords on the Island, owning between them 16 of the 67 lots.

The true contradictions on the Island are explained in the following report from Selkirk's agent, Angus McAuley, a supporter of the Loyal Electors in 1814. "I wished to serve you and the people, it was impossible. The bulk of the inhabitants on this island consist of entrapped loyalists and illiterate Roman Catholic highlanders, the latter floating over the face of the country like Scythiens, without money, bed-clothes, or permanent building for residence ... "[3]

Despite the oppressive conditions, resistance grew among the people and the Loyal Electors continued to work underground. When the charge of malpractice was brought against Palmer, the Compact could not make it stick. By 1817 he was attorney for almost every merchant as well as many small landlords. No small reason for this was the fact that the only other two lawyers on the Island were employed by John Hill who owned 100,000 acres in Prince County. Hill, once a brave fighter against the Compact, turned to support it because he was threatened by the Loyal Electors escheat demands.

Support for the Loyal Electors came from many classes. Thomas Tremlett, who replaced Colclaugh as Chief Justice, was a supporter. When the militia rebelled in 1815, three companies were disbanded and the non-commissioned officers were brought before the Supreme Court. Tremlett, because of popular pressure and his own sympathies, let them go with a trivial fine. The Compact was desperate. Captain James Bagnall, a Compact supporter, reported "that the rapid culture of evil with its progression has been fostered with such care in the community that the uninformed ... have formed the most extravagant notions of their respective stations and duties."[4]

Chapter Notes

1. In Frank MacKinnon, *The Government of Prince Edward Island*, Toronto, U of T Press, 1951, p. 54.
2. In Stanley B. Ryerson, *The Founding of Canada: Beginnings to 1815,* Toronto, Progress Books, 1963.
3. "Selkirk Papers", PAC, M.G. 19, E1, Vol 73, "Angus M. McAulay—Lord Selkirk", October 3, 1814.
4. PAC., M.G. 11, C.O. 226, "Capt. James Bagnall Report", January 25, 1816.

8

Land monopolies
and big business

Life of the Early Settlers

> Saturday the 18th ... At making my poor wife a Windsor
> Chair, and she began her labour.
> November 19th ... My poor wife was safely delivered, Bless
> God, of a daughter.
> November 27 ... At finishing of great chair.
> November 29 ... About 10 o'clock in the forenoon our poor
> baby dies.[1]

Life was hard for the early pioneers. Every member of the
family had to work hard to provide the basic necessities of life.
Farm families in the early 1800's had to be almost entirely self-
sufficient.

Most of their clothing was made on the farm. In spring the
sheep were shorn. The wool was gathered to be washed in a large
iron pot heated over an open fire, dried in the sun, picked free of
chaff, burs and seeds, carded, spun and woven into cloth. The
latter were usually done around the cottage fire in the long winter
evenings. Shirts and pants, socks and mittens, coats and dresses
were all knitted or made from this homespun. The bark of oak
and hemlock trees, when boiled and mixed with the juices of different kinds of lichen, provided dyes.

Quilts and blankets were also made from the wool. Mats and
rugs were hooked from strips cut from worn out blankets and
clothing. Island women are still noted for their patchwork quilts

and brightly coloured home-hooked mats and rugs.

While most tenant farmers were skilled with their hands and made much of the furniture for their own homes, each community had its own furniture maker and carpenter shop. Despite small markets and crude tools, these early craftsmen took pride in their work. The furniture they made was strong, durable, practical and of very high workmanship. Much of it is still in use today.

The work of the community carpenter, or wheelwright as he was called, was quite diversified. This entry for March, 1840, from the diary of Robert Sharpe, my great grandfather, offers us an interesting look into the skills of these workmen.

March 1840 [2]

2nd	John Golde, 3 hours	18th	ditto
	Mrs. Newell	19th	ditto
3rd	Coffin, infirmary	20th	M. Graham,
4th	Making a coffin		making two doors
5th	Spouts [making]	21st	ditto
6th	M. Thorburn, gate	23rd	M. Lookup,
7th	ditto		repairing frames
9th	M. Thorburn, gate	24th	M. Irving
10th	Harrow [making]	25th	Making a boat
11th	Making spouts	26th	ditto
12th	ditto	27th	ditto
13th	M. Thorburn, gate	28th	ditto
14th	Making two coffins	29th	ditto
	infirmary	30th	M. Irving,
16th	Cutting two trees		making a boat
17th	Making a dresser	31st	ditto

Almost all of the food was produced on the family farm. In spring the whole family set about planting the crops: potatoes, corn, wheat, oats and barley. A few cattle, pigs and chickens were raised to provide meat.

Each family had a vegetable garden. A few potatoes and some grain could be sold or traded with local merchants to purchase salt, sugar, molasses, rum and other goods that had to be imported. Because there was no refrigeration and fresh foods were not available during the winter, vegetables and berries were canned or pickled each fall for winter use. Salt fish, cured meat and potatoes rounded out the winter diet.

Island Furniture: *Above, a welt chair hand crafted by an Island carpenter. (PAPEI). Below, a hand crafted couch, a typical piece of furniture in an Island home. (PAPEI).*

Rents, when they were paid, were paid from the small return
from the produce sale or in kind (direct turn-over of produce to
the landlord).

By the early 1800's, most of the land granted in 1767 had come
into the hands of British speculators who had bought it from the
original owners. They held it until roads and new settlers improved its value, then resold it to wealthy British capitalists, such
as Lord Selkirk, John Cambridge and Charles Worrell.

Land Ownership[3]		
	1817	1823
Total number of lots	67	67
Original grantees	7	2½
John Cambridge	9	9½
Lord Selkirk	7	8½
John Hill	5	3½
Stephen Sullivan	4	4
Charles Worrell	3½	5½
Robert Montgomery	2½	5
Others	29	28½

In 1817, 36½ lots were owned by 8 landlords
In 1823, 36 lots were owned by 6 landlords,
46 lots by just 11 landlords

Lumbering and Shipbuilding

In the first quarter of the 18th century a lumber and shipbuilding
industry developed on the Island. Britain was a nation of large
trading companies which exploited the colonies to provide British
merchants with materials to sell in the home market. Britain and
her colonies were widely separated by thousands of miles of water.
To carry on trade, Britain built a large navy and a mighty fleet of
trading ships.

When Europe was blockaded during the Napoleonic wars in
1807, Britain was cut off from her traditional timber supplies in
Scandinavia, forcing her to turn to the North American colonies,
including P.E.I.

Absentee landlords like John Cambridge, and some resident
landlords, were quick to seize on this new opportunity.

Building a Schooner: *Note the men in suits, the bosses, overseeing the work being done. (Private Collection).*

The land being rich with timber, the landlords brought out new settlers from Britain, rented them land, and offered them the "opportunity" of paying their rents by cutting lumber and working in the shipyards. The value of this labour was rated so low however that it was insufficient to pay the rents. The landlords demanded additional payments in cash, which the tenants seldom had. Consequently they sank into debt to the landlords. The introduction of new industry did little to change the feudal system.

Representatives of large merchant companies in Britain were also quick to take advantage of the war situation. William Ellis, with his partner, T.B. Chantes, bought land and set up a shipbuilding operation at Bideford on Malpeque Bay in 1814. He too brought out settlers who became his tenants and workers. The few tenants who were able to secure title to their land were soon indebted to Ellis' company.

By 1815 a number of settlers had succeeded in purchasing land either by paying installments to agreeing landlords after they came to the Island or by direct purchase from landlords before leaving Britain. This was particularly true in the area around Bideford where a group of highland Scots had settled.

In 1818, James Yeo from Cornwall, England, came to work for Ellis as a labourer in the shipyard. He was soon to become one of the most hated men on the Island. Yeo was poor when he arrived, but he worked hard and built up savings by not collecting his wages from the company. After a number of years he asked for the £900 owing him. Since the company did not have enough cash, it offered him the debts on its books as settlement for his wages. The Ellises had written off many of the debts by binding the farmers to their service rather than foreclosing on their land.

The ambitious James Yeo had other ideas! In a series of court actions he took possession of mortgaged land, forcing the farmers either to leave or to become his tenants. With the timber on his newly acquired land, Yeo started his own shipbuilding operation which quickly expanded until he had a number of shipyards in different parts of Prince County.

Another enterprising merchant from Plymouth, England,

Sailing Ship: *In full sail.* (*PAPEI*).

James Pope, came on his father's ship to pick up a load of timber at Bedeque. Quickly seeing the opportunity to expand his father's company, he soon returned, bought land and established a ship-building operation on the shores of Bedeque Bay.

Interest in shipbuilding as a profitable business was not limited to the merchant middlemen. Land agents like William Douse, of the Selkirk estate, also took advantage of the lucrative enterprise.

Merchants, shipbuilders and landowners dominated the com-prador government in the Colony and exploited the hinterland and its people for the benefit of the metropolis. Even resident landlords, who had fought with Patterson to establish indepen-dent control of the colony, took the opportunity to get rich quickly and joined the new exploiters. Those who did the productive work, Island tenants, labourers and shipbuilders together with their counterparts in Britain, received a mere 10% of the profits taken. British merchants and landlords took the rest.

Shipbuilding on P.E.I. [4]		
Year	Number built	Total tonnage
1824	23	3415
1826	40	5414
1828	48	5393
1830	34	2156
1832	42	4006
1834	34	4297
1836	35	4330

By the middle of the 1820's, lumber and shipbuilding were the chief industries of the Island. They accounted for three quarters of all exports. But the social structure of the Island's population remained largely unchanged. The landowners continued to dominate; the tenant farmers continued to provide the labour force for the new industries as well as for the land. The export of foodstuffs increased significantly but not to the benefit of the tenant farmers, many of whom passed their farm produce to their landlords in lieu of cash rent payments. The merchants of the Island did of course benefit. That the landlords did goes without saying. Linked to this new industry and increased food produc-tion was a substantial increase in population.

A new class was emerging on the Island. It was composed of the independent merchants, living mostly in Charlottetown. The prosperity of this class depended upon the purchasing power of the Island's tenant farmers and labourers with whom they allied. The independent merchants fought against the feudal system of landholding and against an economy that saw the wealth of the Island being drawn off by the British companies. With the population growing, more land being cleared and an increased variety of products becoming available, this new class of independent merchants grew in strength.

Chapter Notes

1. Benjamine Chappell, "Diary", Confederation Centre Library, Charlottetown. No Pagination.
2. Robert Sharpe, "Diary 1840", Private Collection.
3. PAC., M.G. 11, C.O. 226, records for 1817 and 1823.
4. PAC.,M.G. 11, C.O. 226, "Vessels Built 1824-1837" transmitted January 1840.

9

Education
and public demands

Education

In the early nineteenth century, educational institutions in the British North American colonies were virtually non-existent. Even so, the Island was the only one where education was totally neglected. That this was so is easily explained. In the other colonies, the independent merchants, being longer and better established, started schools in which their children could receive an education, however elementary. On the Island, on the other hand, the landlords and the trading merchants spent much of their time in Britain and had their children educated there. There was no need for the landowners and trading merchants to attend to the education of the children of the rest of the population from whom they wanted nothing but rents and the fruits of their labours. The small independent merchants were only just emerging as a class.

What little education there was, was entirely in the hands of the Catholic Church. There were two Roman Catholic missionary priests on the whole Island and one Church school in Charlottetown—a seminary to prepare young men for the priesthood.

But the increase in population and the growth of the local merchant class required the government to do something. Lt.-Governor Smith came up with the perfect scheme. It would cost neither the Colonial Office nor the trading merchants one cent. The land reserved for the Church of England and for schools, amounting to some 130 acres in each lot, had never been surveyed. Smith had the survey done. He then declared the most valuable portions, those which had been cleared and cultivated by tenant farmers, to be the reserved land, which he confiscated and sold. The tenant farmers were forced to move without compensation.

Educational Expenditure in 1816 [1]				
District	Missionary Teachers		Other Teachers		Total Salaries
	No.	Salaries	No.	Salaries	
Newfoundland	4	800	6	95	895
Nova Scotia	18	3600	23	270	3870
New Brunswick	9	1800	12	140	1940
Cape Breton	1	200	—	—	200
Upper Canada	8	1475	1	20	1495
Lower Canada	5	1015	—	—	1015
P.E.I.	—	—	—	—	—

This time Smith had gone too far. The people turned on him and the Compact with a vengeance. His former ally, John Stewart, seizing the opportunity to gain public support, led the attack.

In 1823 and 1824, mass meetings were held in all three counties. Resolutions were passed listing over 20 charges against Smith. 2,374 men, representing over half of the male population over 21 years of age, signed a petition demanding that he be removed.

Smith retaliated by arresting the leaders from each county. And yet in spite of all his efforts, the resolutions and the petition got through to the Colonial Office. The Colonial Office decided it preferable to remove Smith rather than face open rebellion.

In the end a school system was established with the money raised from the sale of reserve lands. The land monopolists continued to buy up more land. By 1830, 49 of the 67 lots (73% of the land) were owned by just 12 landlords. Nevertheless, in spite of sell-out after sell-out, by fighting every inch of the way, the people were slowly making gains.

Demands: 1825-1832

In each of the British North American colonies, the Assembly fought to achieve power through gaining control of the money raised by taxation in the colony. Not surprisingly, this had also been the way that the British merchants had wrested control from the King in the 17th century.

The Supply Question: By the time the new Lt.-Governor, John Ready, another British colonel, arrived, the struggle for Smith's recall and for expanding trade had moulded the Island petty bourgeoisie and the tenant farmers into a strong force for social change.

Ready made his first mistake when he appointed two big resident landlords, Charles Worrell and William Hill, a brother of former Patterson supporter John Hill to the council. The petty bourgeois-tenant alliance dominated the Assembly. Immediately they passed a resolution which would give the Assembly the sole right to grant and appropriate supplies (money) raised through taxation. The passing of this resolution marked the beginning of 30 years of struggle for "responsible government". The same struggle was being waged at this time in the other British colonies where the farmers and independent merchants were also demanding more and more control over their own affairs.

Land Titles: The Assembly forced an act through the legislature requiring all land deeds to be registered in Charlottetown. By this time the Council and lieutenant-governor dared not openly oppose popular demands. Of course, the landlords opposed the act. They claimed that if there was some "technical dispute" over the title, tenants would not pay rent. The Imperial government, not under direct pressure from the people of the colony, disallowed the act on the grounds that "tenants having once paid a landlord, recognize who owns the land." That numbers of tenants were required to pay rent to two landlords, each claiming title, had no bearing on the question, as far as London was concerned.

Land titles that were not registered allowed the landlords to rob many settlers. There were numerous cases of people buying land from a landlord in England, only to arrive on the Island to find that the land they had paid for was owned by someone else or did not exist at all. The Acadiens paid £1000 toward the purchase of lot 15 only to find that the person they had paid had no title. The legal landlord, when he arrived on the scene, had no sympathy and they were forced to pay him the back rent.

Fishery Reserves: When the land was originally granted, a strip of land along the coast (to a depth of 500 feet above the high water mark) of all lots bordering water was reserved for fisheries. However, landlords of adjacent land paid no attention to this provision and rented the reserve land along with their own. The people demanded that this land be returned to the Crown and reserved for fisheries.

As in Newfoundland, Island residents were discouraged and often prevented from fishing. It was more profitable for British fishing companies to take the fish caught directly back to Britain rather than share the value of the catch with resident fishermen or merchants or allow an independent colonial fishery to develop. Every summer, the British fishing fleets, having fished the waters and dried their catch, sailed back to Britain. They left nothing behind.

Paying the Civil Lits: By 1833, the merchant-tenant alliance demanded that the Island itself raise the money to pay the cost of local government: this cost was called the Civil List. The alliance wanted the Assembly to control the Civil List so that the lieutenant-governor would need the approval of the Assembly to pay the salaries of government employees. Up to this time they had been paid by the Colonial Office.

It was proposed that the money be raised by taxing the landlords through a land tax. The Council agreed that the Island should pay the Civil List but not at the expense of the landlords. The landlords proposed for their part that the Island be annexed to Nova Scotia to cut out the expense of a separate administration.

When the Colonial Office refused to give assent to an act passed by the Assembly, the workers and tenants in Kings County took matters into their own hands.

Chapter Notes

1. PAC., M.G. 11, C.O. 226, "State of Missions" transmitted October 1816.

10

The fight for land

The Tenants Organise

The tenants of north eastern Kings County had been resisting the
landlords for years, refusing to pay rent or take out leases.

In 1819, Edward Abell, the land agent for James Townshend,
the son of Field Marshall Lord Townshend who had succeeded
Wolfe as commander-in-chief after the siege of Québec was killed
by Patrick Pierce, a tenant on lot 56.

The incident occurred when Abell's wife tried to buy a beauti-
ful black carriage horse from Pierce. Pierce refused to sell. Mrs.
Abell prevailed upon her husband to demand immediate payment
of rent and to take the horse if Pierce failed to pay. Pierce went
among his neighbours to raise the cash. He returned with the
payment in Spanish coins to find Abell with a constable sitting on
the woodpile holding the horse. Pierce offered the money but
Abell refused it because it was not British sterling. Pierce then
went into his house and brought out a musket with bayonet
attached and shot Abel twice. Although a £20,000 reward was
offered for his capture, Pierce was hidden by his fellow tenants
until he was able to escape to one of the other colonies.

With this kind of solidarity in their ranks, the tenants continued to organise resistance to the land agents as occasion
demanded. From this local base they expanded until, by 1830, the
tenants' movement encompassed all the northern and eastern
parts of Kings County.

The movement had as its objective the establishment of an
Escheat Court which would have the power to confiscate the land
of owners who failed to meet the conditions governing the original
granting of the land. Until the Court was set up, the tenants
decided to withhold their rents.

The only previously organised attempt to take ownership of the
land away from the landlords had been through the Society of
Loyal Electors. For thirty years the efforts of men like J. B. Palmer
had brought little relief for the farmers. They still had to pay rent
and still had no title to their land. Now they had the strength and
leadership to form their own party, the Escheat Party, and to elect
their own men to the Assembly. They combined electoral politics
with militant resistance to prevent the landlords from taking their
land or property or collecting their rents.

The leader of the movement was William Cooper. Cooper had
arrived on the Island in 1818 at the age of 33. He was born in
England on November 4, 1786, ran away to sea at age 11, served
with Nelson at the Battle of Trafalgar, and subsequently sailed
the seven seas as a ship captain.

Cooper settled near Bay Fortune on a farm which he named
Sailor's Hope. There he built a home and took to stock raising.
He also erected a grist mill and built ships.

On February 26, 1820, James Townshend appointed Cooper to
succeed Abell as his agent. In this job he was particularly successful. He succeeded in getting 60 tenants to sign leases—a
major achievement among settlers who did not recognise the
claims of the landlords and who considered the land their own.

Moreover, Townshend's terms were comparatively harsh. In a
colony in which the usual lease ran for some 999 years, Cooper
was instructed to let land lying contiguous to the sea shore for a
period not exceeding 84 years, and land more than five miles
inland for not more than 200 years. Townshend also demanded
that each tenant pay half the cost of executing his own lease.

By 1829, nine years after his appointment, Cooper had become
so disgusted and appalled at the way tenants were being treated
that he joined and became a leader of the tenants' movement.

William Cooper: *The leader of the Escheat Party. (PAPEI).*

Our Country's Freedom and Farmer's Right

In 1831, Cooper ran for election to the Assembly in a by-election under the banner "Our Country's Freedom and Farmer's Right". He was bitterly opposed by Angus MacDonald who was the landlords' candidate and a protegé of Charles Worrell, a major landlord in northern Kings County. When it became obvious at the open polling booth that Cooper would win the election, Worrell, Macdonald and their cohorts attempted to prevent it by creating a riot, disrupting the voting procedure and forcing the returning officer to close the poll early.

In spite of their efforts the Assembly later confirmed Cooper's election by a margin of one vote.

In the Assembly, Cooper demanded that a court of Escheat be set up. "The more I consider the question," he said, "the more plain it appears that nothing less than a general Escheat will do justice to, or satisfy the inhabitants of this Island."[1] To support his position he gave the following concise account of the people's struggle:

> ... did the grantees settle the land within the time limit with any description of people? No. Did they use or occupy the land themselves? No. Then why did they wish to hold the lands they could not use nor occupy? It was not the lands they wanted, but by holding the land, to have a claim on the labour of their fellow subjects, who had equal rights with themselves [under the law]. About the close of the American war of 1780, the Grantees gave up part of the land to government to settle the American Loyalists, and in a short time reclaimed it again, and now hold the greater part of it. After His Majesty reduced the Quit Rent from six shillings per 100 acres, to two shillings, so that some part of it might be paid, the Grantees, by petition, signified that the country was too poor to pay any Quit Rent, but demanded Five Pounds yearly rent of the tenantry for the same quantity of land;—Thus, when His Majesty reduced the Quit Rent to the Grantees, they in proportion raised the rent to the tenantry; when His Majesty extended the time limited for the fulfillment of the conditions to the Grantees, they shortened the terms of the lease to the tenantry from 999 years to 84 and 40 years.[2]

Cooper then elaborated on the economics behind the leasehold tenure system on the Island and the benefactors thereof:

His Majesty's subjects in the neighbouring Colonies can have a grant forever for £15 or thereabout for 100 acres of land, and that sum to be applied for the benefit and improvement of the country they live in; but His Majesty's subjects in this colony must pay a sum of £15 every third year, to be withdrawn from the Island, and pay taxes for every improvement and pay support of the Government; besides this, the tax burthened people of England must pay our Officers of Government, and the tenantry of this land in the midst of privations and misery, must pay a yearly tax of from Five to Ten Pounds to keep up the aristocracy of England.[3]

He further argued that "Property is the labour of Man", that the tenants "have wasted their youth in clearing lands for others, they have planted their labour where the forests grow, they have made a garden in the wilderness, and built a cabin where the bear has his den."[4]

"If it is to be admitted," said Cooper, "that labour is money, and money is power, then wealth collected by avarice, extortion, and fraud, to a great amount, and wielded by craft and deceit, might crush the liberties of mankind. ... There cannot be a greater monopoly of the labour of man than by holding the possession of large tracts of land."[5]

Therefore Cooper argued "if the grantees did not fulfill their conditions, it [the land] must become forfeit to the Crown, to enable government to grant it to those subjects that did settle on the land and fulfill the conditions."[6]

Although the Escheat motion was vetoed by the Colonial Office, in the years 1832-33 the tenants persisted in their organising.

Population 1833   32,292

In the week of January 8, 1834, the *Royal Gazette* carried this story: "On Sunday June 8, 1834, the Deputy Sheriff and Peace Officers well armed left Charlottetown to issue warrants against accused in Kings County who refused to come to court. When the party arrived they encountered a large group of settlers armed with spears, pitch forks and muskets who refused to let them issue warrants saying they would die to a man first."[7]

This well-organised resistance prevented the landlords, their agents or the Sheriff from collecting the rents or issuing warrants. By late 1834, the whole eastern part of Kings County was under the control of the tenants—out of bounds to the landlords, their agents and comprador supporters in Charlottetown. It was a Liberated Area.

The tenants in the Liberated Area carried on a successful trade with U.S. fishermen and British merchant ships: trading bait and foodstuff for consumer necessities. For a number of years the social and economic life of the Liberated Area was carried on independently of the colonial government in Charlottetown. At the time it was illegal for the U.S. fishermen to fish the Island's waters. However, neither the colonial government nor the British could any more regulate the fishing than they could collect rents.

In 1834, Cooper was joined in the Assembly by more members of the Escheat Party. Among them was the fiery activist, John McIntosh, the son of a Scottish immigrant born in Mill Cove in 1791 and John LaLacheur, also a native Islander, both of whom were to become leaders of the Escheat movement. Cooper continued to lead with the zeal of a convert.

Hay River Meeting

Despite the victories achieved by direct militant action and in the Assembly, the feudal system of tenure continued to be the law. Rents continued to be collected although they were fewer in number as the Liberated Area expanded year by year. On December 18, 1836, the tenants massed at Hay River near Souris to decide on political action. They passed resolutions and sent a petition to King William IV demanding that a court of Escheat be set up and that they be given protection from the landlords, their agents and their friends in the compact. Raising the cry of "law and order", heard so often today, the Lt. Governor and the Council declared the resolutions treasonous. Let's look at two of them:

Resolution No. 3
Resolved that the representations just read in the draft of

the petition to His Majesty, and agreed to by this meeting, are truths which cannot be contravened, exhibit a scene of fraud, deceit, and oppression, on the part of the grantees and land monopolists, against the inhabitants of this Island, which, in the opinion of religious and reasonable men, is wickedness in the sight of God, derogatory to the honor and dignity of the King, and the British Nation, and subversive to the sacred right of property; that longer to pay rent to such landlords, under such circumstances and after our repeated prayers for justice, is to foster oppression and reward crime.

> *Resolution No. 4*
> That this meeting is moved by sacred obligation of religion, by the honor and dignity of the King and the British Nation, by the rights of men to the fruits of their labour by justice and equity (the basis of good government and civilized society), to preserve from the distress of such landlords the fruits of our industry, raised for the maintenance of our families, until his majesty is informed of the true situation and condition of his subjects in this Island, and his decision obtained according to the merits of the case.[8]

The tenants had complete faith in the justice of the British Monarch. They believed that the unscrupulous government officials and landlords of whom the King knew nothing, were their only enemies. They reasoned that if they presented their plight to the King they would receive justice.

The meeting further demanded that:

1. The combination of land monopolies be broken up. (Not only had large amounts of land come under the ownership of a few large landlords, but absentee landlords in London had formed the P.E.I. Association to ensure that the Colonial Office rejected any measures taken in the colony which threatened their interests.)

2. That land be given to the Loyalists. (Most of the Loyalists' grants given by Gov. Patterson in 1784 had been returned to the original owners so the Loyalists lived on land without titles.)

3. That a new Assembly be elected. (The tenants now felt that they had the strength to elect a majority to the Assembly.)

Most tenants continued to resist their landlords by withholding their rents. Cooper, however, continued paying his rent to Townshend, although not regularly. By making these payments he guaranteed the security of his own farm while the only security his neighbours had was their steadfast unity of defiance.

Threatening the Establishment

The militancy of the tenants frightened Lt.-Governor John Harvey. He suggested a compromise: landlords should refrain from collecting back rent. The landlords' reply was to tell him that the government had no right to interfere in matters of private property. And once again, in spite of the almost total disregard for the terms set down in the original grants the Imperial government ruled against the tenants.

By 1835, J.B. Palmer had sold out to the Charlottetown establishment. Having been unable to beat the Compact, he had found it in his interest to join them. During the thirty years since he had led the Loyal Electors he had become increasingly rich and influential, representing large landlords as legal council and land agent. In 1835, as leader of the majority party in the Assembly—the Compact—he opposed any move that would threaten the status quo.

When the Assembly met in February 1836, following the Hay River meeting, Cooper, McIntosh and LaLacheur apologized to the Assembly for their actions at Hay River. They said "the resolutions adopted at Hay River were not intended to convey sentiment to resist the law and authority of government—that they were sorry for having used words and favoring measures which were considered by the Lt.-Governor and the House as illegal and humbly apologize."[9]

The Compact was not satisfied. It demanded an apology which would have had the three admit gross misrepresentation of the House on the question of Escheat and therefore guilty of a breach of parliamentary privilege. They refused and the House voted 9-4 against acceptance of the original apology. They were then expelled.

Two sessions later the Escheaters were readmitted when a lawyer from Nova Scotia successfully pleaded their case. No lawyer on the Island would confront the Compact.

Nevertheless the tenants' movement and the demand for Escheat grew. On December 24, 1836, tenants from Murray River,
Guernsey Cove and White Sands in southern Kings County met
and unanimously adopted the address and resolutions passed at
the Hay River meeting over a year earlier.

Revolution in the Canadas

While the colonial rulers were under attack on the Island, unrest
and revolution were also prevalent in the Canadas. Here the
growing strength of the small merchants class in alliance with
farmers and small craftsmen also challenged the colonial
rulers—in Lower Canada called the *Chateau Clique*—in Upper
Canada the *Family Compact*.

In Lower Canada the reformers were French patriots organised
into the *Parti Canadien* led by Louis Joseph Papineau. In Upper
Canada the reformers were led by William Lyon Mackenzie.

In the fall of 1837 the struggle broke into armed rebellion when
the patriots were attacked by British troops and Mackenzie's
forces launched an attack on Toronto, the headquarters of the
Family Compact.

The outcome was defeat for both the Upper and Lower Canadian reformers. The repression of the British was ugly. Twenty-
one prisoners of war were executed in Upper Canada where there
were 885 arrests for high treason and insurrection. Thousands of
people fled the colonies for exile in the United States and hundreds of prisoners were transported to the British prison colony in
Tasmania.

In spite of the defeat, the revolution was not a complete failure.
The Family Compact and its counterpart, the Chateau Clique and
their network of local despots were badly shaken. The British realised that changes had to take place if renewed revolution was to
be avoided.

In May, 1838, Lord Durham, the son of a wealthy coal mine
owner, was sent to the colonies as Governor-General and High
Commissioner to enquire into the state of affairs. Durham was a
leader of the Whig party in England which was the party of the

rising industrial bourgeoisie.*

Chapter Notes

1. "House of Assembly Debates", March 27, 1832 reported in *Royal Gazette*, April 3, 1832.
2. *Ibid.*
3. *Ibid.*
4. *Ibid.*
5. *Ibid.*
6. *Ibid.*
7. *Royal Gazette*, January 8, 1834, (week of).
8. PAC., M.G. 11, C.O. 226, contained in letter from Colonial Secretary's office to Cooper, LaLacheur and McIntosh.
9. "House of Assembly Debates", January 1836.

*In England the new industrial development had concentrated manufacturing into large companies with large work forces. The merchant traders of an earlier period now became industrial capitalists. Craftsmen became paid employees of the big industries.

11

Victory and defeat

Lord Durham's Report

Durham attributed the "unrest" on the Island to the land agents and the leasehold tenure system. He reported that "Against this system, this small and powerless community has in vain been struggling for some years; a few active and influential proprietors [landlords] in London have been able to drown the remonstrances, and defeat the efforts of a distant and petty province." He saw the Island as a potential granary for the British colonies and attributed the lack of development to the landlords "who would neither promote nor permit its cultivation."[1]

While Durham remonstrated about the "plight" of the Island people, he recommended in the vaguest terms that the abuses be removed. The only real solution was to turn the land over to the people who tilled it—the Island tenants. However, such a recommendation posed a threat to the existing laws governing private property. Durham could not offer such a recommendation because the class whose interests he represented depended for its wealth and power on ownership of private property.

But the "distant and petty" people were not as powerless as Durham reported. By 1838, the Island tenants had established a large Liberated Area. Here power was in the hands of the people, a concept foreign to a man like Durham who saw power always in the hands of an elite.

The history of the Escheat Party and William Cooper's political career both reached a peak in 1838 when 18 of the 24 Assembly seats were won by Escheat Party candidates.

When the House met in January 1839, it elected Cooper speaker by a vote of 16-6. With their clear mandate, the party introduced legislation that would end the leasehold tenure system. Resolutions called for:

The Establishment of an Escheat Court: The court would have power to take the land from those landlords who had not fulfilled the conditions of the grants and return it to the crown. The land could then be turned over to the tenants who tilled it. Since, argued Cooper, property is the labour of man, those whose labour cleared and cultivated the land would have legal ownership of it.

A Tax of Wilderness Land: The tax would encourage landlords either to sell uncultivated land or to bring it under cultivation.
Land Grants to the Loyalists: The grants would give loyalist settlers legal title to the land they tilled.
The Return of Fishery Reserves to the Crown: Although Islanders fished very little, and had been discouraged from doing so, the Escheat party wanted to encourage the industry and at the same time further harass the landlords.

The Assembly sessions of 1839, '40 and '41 passed the resolutions. Each time they were rejected by either the Council or the Colonial Office.

In Nova Scotia, over a million acres of land held by landlords had been escheated and either turned over or sold to the tenants. The greater strength of the merchants in Nova Scotia had forced this solution but in P.E.I. the greatest influence on the Colonial Office still came from the landlords' lobby in London.

In 1839 the Assembly sent Cooper to London to confront the Colonial Secretary, John Russell. When he arrived, Russell refused to see him. Cooper wrote Russell a number of letters explaining why he had come and requesting to be heard. It was not until he returned to the Island, without seeing Russell, that he learned that the Lieutenant Governor had received a letter from Russell's secretary which said: "The subject to which your [Cooper's] letters refer could not be properly discussed between his lordship and a delegate from the House of Assembly in Prince Edward Island, either in written or oral communications, and the views of His Majesty respecting them will be communicated through the regular channels of official correspondence with that office."[2]

The tenantry now lost all hope of justice from the Colonial Office or the entrenched colonials in Charlottetown and gave up on the electoral process. In 1841, Lt.-Governor Fitzroy dissolved the Assembly. In 1842, the Escheat Party held only its Kings County seats. The majority in the new Assembly was held by the Family Compact led by Edward Palmer, Joseph Pope, James Yeo and William Douse.

Cooper, McIntosh and LaLacheur all won re-election and continued to sit in the Assembly.

Expanding the Liberated Zone

After defeat at the polls, the Escheat Party and the tenants turned with renewed energy to strengthen and expand their Liberated Area.

In March 1843, a surveyor was sent to East Point to mark out the boundaries of unleased land where the tenants had been cutting firewood. A group of some 200 residents drove him away, tore up the markers and burned the house of the landlord's agent who had sent him. The landlord's friends in Charlottetown responded by sending the sheriff and 30 civil constables to arrest the identified "rioters". Fifteen military regulars of the British army armed with rifles occupied St. Margaret's and a similar force occupied Souris. A military reserve of 70 men was sent to St. Peter's to be ready for any organised resistance. A reward of £200 was offered to any witness who would testify.

However, no witnesses came forward; the tenants were not to be bribed. Neither did they make the mistake of confronting the British army. They simply hid the people for whom the sheriff had warrants, forcing him to return to Charlottetown empy-handed. The tenants typically used such tactics to confuse and humiliate the superior forces of the landlords and the British. The civil force even when backed by the British army was neither big enough nor

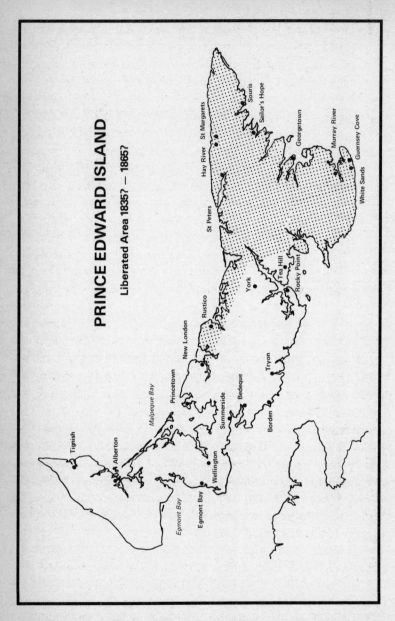

PRINCE EDWARD ISLAND
Liberated Area 1835? — 1865?

Tignish

Alberton

Malpeque Bay

Princetown

New London

Rustico

St Peters

Hay River

St Margarets

Souris

Sailor's Hope

Georgetown

Murray River

Guernsey Cove

White Sands

York

Tea Hill

Rocky Point

Tryon

Bedeque

Summerside

Borden

Wellington

Egmont Bay

Egmont Bay

<u>Liberated Area:</u> *The area referred to in the text at its greatest extent in 1843. The place names include both those used in 1843 and those used today.*

mobile enough to search every root cellar or barn where the tenants might hide their friends.

John MacDonald, the parish priest at St. Margaret's, was suspected of calling in the troops. John McIntosh and another elder requested Father MacDonald to call a meeting of the congregation and give a full explanation of his involvement. The meeting was held in MacDonald's absence and a new group of Church elders was elected. During Mass next Sunday, MacDonald refused to recognize the new elders and McIntosh rose to his feet and demanded an explanation of MacDonald's actions.

In the midst of the disturbance, MacDonald knelt at the altar and asked for peace; he later charged McIntosh for interrupting a service of divine worship. When the case came before the county court in Georgetown, it was dismissed because no law which covered it could be found. The popular cry for MacDonald's removal was instant and St. Margaret's soon had a new spiritual adviser.

In the 1840's the Island was divided between the Liberated Area lying north and east of Charlottetown which was controlled by the tenants, and the city and the remaining rural area which was controlled by the landlords. When the land agents and sheriffs ventured into the Liberated Area they were greeted by the echoing wail of the *conch* shell as the first tenant to see the intruders signalled a warning to his neighbours.

The economy of the Liberated Area was carried on entirely separately from the rest of the Island. Cooper and others built ships which sailed to Britain, the United States and the West Indies to trade farm produce for needed consumer goods, the conch shells and luxury items like rum. This, combined with trade with passing fishing boats and British vessels, kept the tenants well supplied.

In March 1843, tenants in New London, in Queen's County met and voted to join the eastern tenants and withhold their rent. They passed the following resolution:

> That the government of this colony, unlike the government of any other colony, did not govern for the benefit of the majority of the people but for the benefit of a couple of dozen land speculators, thus conscious dependents and

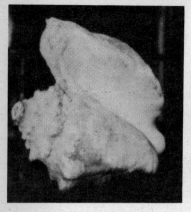
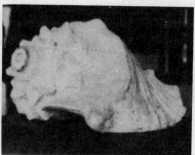

Conch Shell: *First the end was cut off to leave a hole. Then by blowing into the hollow shell in much the same manner as one would blow into a trumpet, a loud shrill noise was produced. This sound could be heard for miles.*

parasites.[3]

The chairman of the New London meeting, Duncan McLeod, a local tenant, was later arrested and charged with libel. He was never brought to trial because a jury of his peers could not be found to convict him.

At Mount Stewart and East Point in the northwest; Belfast in the southeast; Rocky Point across the harbour from Charlottetown; Princetown on Malpeque Bay and New London on the north shore, land agents and special constables heard the frightening wail of the conch rallying tenants armed with pitch forks, rocks and muskets to drive them back to Charlottetown.

By the end of 1843 the borders of the Liberated Area extended from New London across the north shore through New Glasgow and Oyster Bed Bridge; then southeast, north of Charlottetown to Pownell. The area north and east of this border was under the control of the tenants.

Chapter Notes

1. Gerald M. Craig (ed.), *Lord Durham's Report*, Carleton Library Series, Toronto, McClelland and Stewart, 1963, pp. 107-8.
2. PAC., M.G. 11, C.O. 226, "Russell to Fitzroy", July 24, 1839.
3. PAC., M.G. 11, C.O. 226, "Huntley to Stanley", July 24, 1843.

12

Responsible government

The New Reformers

While the tenants were strengthening their position in the countryside, a new reform movement was taking shape in the Assembly.

In 1842, George Coles at the age of 32 was elected in New London. He entered the Assembly as a Compact candidate but soon fell out with the Compact when he failed to get their support for measures which would end the leasehold tenure system.

Coles was born on the Island on September 20, 1810, the son of James and Sarah Coles who farmed in Charlottetown Royalty. When he entered the Assembly, in addition to his farm, he had a very successful brewery and distillery in Charlottetown. He was one of a growing group of Island businessmen whose interests lay on the Island. This group opposed people like Pope, Palmer, Yeo and Douse who made their fortunes as middlemen in the feudal leasehold tenure system and as representatives of British merchants.

By 1842, everyone except the leaders and supporters of the Escheat Party accepted the argument that since most of the land had changed hands several times, the landlords with title were the legal owners and not subject to Escheat. Coles considered the proposals of the Escheat party unworkable because they would not be approved by London and undesirable because they would threaten the legal status of private property. As a manufacturer and an independent capitalist, it was in his interest, and in the interest of his class, to defend property rights. But also it was in his interest to increase the purchasing power of the tenants by freeing them from the landlords.

When Lt.-Governor Huntley, a moderate, was sent by the Colonial Office to replace Fitzroy, he was instructed to settle the conflict over land. He refused to take orders from the Family Compact and consequently the Compact-controlled Assembly voted non-confidence in him. He retaliated by dissolving the Assembly in 1846.

The ensuing election campaign was bitterly fought. In the Belfast district, John MacDougall and John Small, candidates for the Escheat Party and now supporters of Coles, were declared elected. Douse and MacLean, the Compact candidates, challenged their election on the grounds that there had been intimidation at the polls and a by-election was called for March 1, 1847.

On the day of the by-election, fighting broke out at the Pinette poll when the supporters of MacDougall and Small, both of whom were Irish Catholic tenants, were attacked by the Scotch protestant supporters of Douse and MacLean. Three people were killed and a number injured before the poll was closed and the riot brought under control. Two weeks later, on March 19, the election was held again under the protection of Sheriff Cundell and his constables. Douse and MacLean were elected by acclamation.

The Belfast Riot was a clash between those who wanted reform and those who wanted to maintain the status quo. That support for the two positions divided along religious lines was a secondary matter but undoubtedly it added fuel to the fire. Although Douse and MacLean were elected in Belfast the challenge of the Island bourgeoisie could not be denied. Concessions had to be made if the present system was to be saved.

Coles and his supporters, who formed the core of the Reform Party, won a majority in the new Assembly. Among the reformers were Alexander Rae, a former member of the Escheat Party, and

George Coles: *Leader of the fight for responsible government and the first Premier of Prince Edward Island.* (PAPEI).

Edward Whelan, a young journalist who had been sent to the
Island by Joseph Howe of Nova Scotia at the request of the reformers to start a newspaper. His paper, the *Palladium*, became
the chief vehicle and party newspaper of the reformers.

In the new Assembly the members immediately passed resolutions demanding responsible government. They proposed that
half the Executive Council, heretofore appointed from the Legislative Council, be appointed from the majority party in the
Assembly.

Lt.-Governor Huntley and his predecessor Fitzroy were accused
by the Assembly of protecting the interests of landlords and
British merchants in land ownership disputes.

When Coles sought approval from his constituents for his
appointment to the Council in a by-election in 1st Queens in
August 1847, he was bitterly opposed by the Compact. The
Examiner, which succeeded the Palladium, reported on August
14, that "The Black Watch [Family Compact] took the field in
full force, and confident of victory, not a man was wanting. From
their dark-looking Colonel Pope, down to the meanest slave and
servant of their wills, all were furiously zealous in their attempt to
drive Mr. Coles from the field. All their efforts proved abortive
and they themselves in the end were forced to sound a retreat."[1]

Coles' victory celebration in Charlottetown lasted all night and
exuberant Coles' supporters went about the city breaking windows of Compact supporters.

To appoint Coles to the Executive Council might be a useful
political tactic but to permit the Assembly to exercise the full
powers of government would be a major strategic error. It was not
surprising, therefore, to find Lt.-Governor Huntley writing to
London that he was opposed to "concentrating the whole government power in the Assembly, where there is neither, nor do I
think for a long time yet, any sufficient intelligence to govern at
all."[2]

But even the concession of Coles' appointment was enough to
outrage the absentee landlords in London. When Huntley's term
of office expired later in 1847, they lobbied to keep him from
being appointed another term. Although the Island Assembly

we are indebted to Mrs. Bayfield for recording what our capital looked like in an earlier day.

Old Market Square, by the same lady.

Charlottetown: *Sketches of street scenes in the capital circa 1860. (PA-PEI).*

petitioned for his re-appointment, the landlord lobbyists won the day. Coles resigned from the Council to devote his energies to being full time leader and organiser of the new Reform Party.

Sir Donald Campbell, the landlords' choice, succeeded Huntley. Campbell was totally opposed to any concessions leading to responsible government. His appointment followed a well considered policy of the Colonial Office of alternating moderates and tyrants in rebellious colonies. This practice was calculated to buy time by raising the people's hopes of reform and then grinding them under the tyrant's heel when none were forthcoming.

Campbell, like Huntley, argued that only a few in Charlottetown (members of the Compact) were fit to hold government office. "In order for a community to be fit to receive a responsible government system," he wrote to the Colonial Office, "it is essential that it should, not in the capital or one particular town alone, but diffused throughout the whole extent, have individuals possessed of property, educated and intelligent, in such a number to ensure that whatever political party should from time to time gain ascendency in the Assembly, its ranks will always be able to furnish men desirous of devising useful measures capable of conducting the government, and to whom, from their respectability, the administration of the affairs of the colony may be safely entrusted." [3]

The same arguments were used to oppose responsible government in the other North American colonies. However, in 1848, Nova Scotia, with a larger independent bourgeoisie than the Island, followed by New Brunswick and the Canadas in 1849, got responsible government. In P.E.I. it was not to be denied. George Coles had become a popular and dynamic leader. He and other independent capitalists had established a solid manufacturing base on the Island. He, not Campbell, had the support of the people.

Campbell in his remonstrations to the Colonial Office now had to state the truth if he was going to stem the tide toward responsible government. "Responsible government would return those people who would fight for Escheat and thus eliminate other capable people who might run the government. The tenantry rep-

Home of the Rich: *While most Islanders lived in frame, often one-room houses, the comprador government officials and landlord agents lived in mansions such as this. (PAPEI).*

The Cunards

Many of these merchant-landlords got their initial capital for bigger investments from exploiting Island tenants and workers. One of the most notable was Samuel Cunard, an Englishman, who bought his first land in 1838 and by the 1860's had amassed holdings of 212,000 acres, almost 15% of the land on the island. The Cunard family combined this with huge lumber concessions in the Miramichi region of New Brunswick to establish the Cunard shipping lines. By the mid 1800's he had established a virtual monopoly on steam shipping in the North Atlantic. They later moved from Halifax to Boston where a greater volume of trade meant greater profits. From there they built one of the largest shipping lines in the world. Such ships as the passenger liner Queen Elizabeth were owned by the Cunard lines.

resents 4 / 5 of the people and political power [under responsible government] rests in their hands: which has been increased with the introduction of Irish paupers who have brought with them their feelings of discontent."[4] It was not a matter of the capability of the people but rather a concern for the class interests of the landlords and British merchants. The Imperial government got the point.

No Power, No Pay

In 1848, when the Imperial government demanded that the Island pay its own civil list [salaries of government officials] the reformers passed an act in the Assembly providing for settlement of salaries on a yearly basis in Island currency,* on the condition that the Crown's annual revenue from duties and taxes of £2,000 be turned over to the Assembly.

This act was rejected by the Colonial Office. They were not willing to turn control of Colonial Officials' salaries over to the Assembly. Campbell responded by dissolving the Assembly. He expressed the hope that the new Assembly "will be responsible enough to separate the question of responsible government from the settlement of the civil list."[5] He hoped to remove the money issue from the Assembly and thus the only club it had to force the introduction of responsible government.

Campbell's attempt to get a more favorable Assembly failed when in 1850 the reformers won the election. In the first session of the new Assembly they demanded that the Executive Council be appointed from the majority party in the Assembly. When Campbell refused, the Assembly, led by Coles and Whelan, refused to appropriate funds for government expenditure and was adjourned at its own request until April 25. It reconvened briefly, refused to vote supply and adjourned for the summer on May 1.

Coles and the reformers had backed Campbell up against the wall but he stubbornly refused to admit defeat. In a last ditch

---

*Island currency was valued lower than the British pound sterling, the currency in which salaries had been paid until this time.

effort, he attempted to change the franchise so that in any election the Compact's Conservative Party would be assured of victory. He proposed that:

    (a) the franchise, at the time almost universal to all males, be limited to freeholders and leaseholders who resided on a maximum of 50 acres for at least 20 years at a minimum rent of 50 shillings, and

    (b) that electoral districts be abolished and that members be elected on a county basis; two members from Charlottetown, five from each county and one each from Georgetown and Princetown.

This scheme would have reduced the number of Assembly seats from 24 to 19 and the electorate from 7,217 to 3,589. But the Imperial government realised that the "jig was up". If P.E.I. was to remain a colony and civil order to be preserved they had to grant responsible government. They had fired their biggest guns but the combined force of the independent merchants, the tenants and increased population was not to be denied.

In the fall of 1850, Duncan Campbell, a defeated man, died in Government House in Charlottetown.

In January 1851, Sir Alexander Bannerman was sent to the Island with instructions to introduce responsible government. In February, the old Executive Council resigned and George Coles became the first premier of Prince Edward Island and the head of a Council picked from the Reform Party which held the majority in the assembly.

Chapter Notes

1. *The Examiner*, August 14, 1847.
2. PAC., M.G. 11, C.O. 226, "Huntley to Grey", May 9, 1847.
3. PAC., M.G. 11, C.O. 226, "Campbell to Grey", June 1, 1848.
4. Ibid.
5. PAC., M.G. 11, C.O. 226, "Campbell to Grey", June 16, 1850.

13

Land reform
at the farmer's expense

New Political Alliance

In 1850, George Coles' Reform Party was renamed the Liberal
Party. It had the support of the Island's bourgeoisie and former
members of the Escheat Party which by this time had ceased to
exist. After his election in 1842, William Cooper, who had led the
Escheat Party in its finest hour in 1838, lost interest in politics. He
did not contest a seat in the 1846 election, choosing to return to
the sea and shipbuilding. In 1844 he built the *Flora Beaton*, in
1845 the *Sea Walker*, in 1846 the *Malvina* and in 1849 the *Packet*.
In the latter, a 182-ton vessel laden with lumber, he and his entire
family, including three daughters and six sons, set sail for the
California gold fields from Sailor's Hope on December 5, 1849.

The Packet sailed around Cape Horn in 230 days, arriving in
San Franciso on July 20, 1850. Shortly after his arrival Cooper
decided to return to the Island by the overland route intent on
selling his property and returning to join his family. While he was
away his wife and other members of his family died of cholera and
Cooper never returned to California. In 1855 he was once again
back in the Assembly, this time as a Liberal but still advocating
escheat. He continued to sit in the Assembly until 1862. He died
on June 10, 1867 at his home at Sailor's Hope.

The party opposed to the Liberals, which was led by the Compact, had become known as the *Conservative Party*. They con-

tinued to use every means at their disposal to hold back change. For them change meant doom. As Coles more than once remarked, the land agents were more intent than the landlords to maintain the status quo.

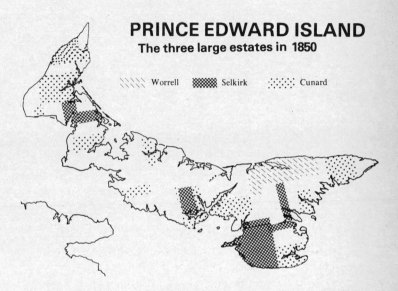

PRINCE EDWARD ISLAND
The three large estates in 1850

\\\\\ Worrell   ▨▨▨ Selkirk   ∷∷ Cunard

The Big Estates: *Map showing the land held by Worrell, Selkirk and Cunard in 1850.*

Confiscation or Expropriation

The new government of Coles' Liberal Party introduced legislation that would bring to an end the Island's land tenure system and thereby relieve the tenant farmers of the burden they had borne for so long. The government introduced legislation that would make Island currency legal tender for paying rents. Yet another bill would require landlords to pay for land improvements made by tenants. All this legislation was disallowed by the Colonial Office because it violated the "rights of property" and the agreements between landlords and tenants. "Responsible" government notwithstanding, the landlords' interests continued to influence London's decisions.

   In 1853, the Liberals finally got an act approved by the Colonial

Office. This was the Land Purchase Act which allowed the Island government to purchase the land of those landlords who were willing to sell and then re-sell the land in small lots to the tenants. The act allowed the Island bourgeoisie to control the purchase and sale of land and did not put in question property rights.

Some Liberals, particularly William Cooper, criticised the government saying that it was spending the people's money to purchase land to which the landlords had not rightful claim or title. The tenants were paying for the land over and over again. First they cleared the land and gave it whatever value it had. Second they paid, through their taxes, when the government purchased the land from the landlords. And finally, they paid when they purchased the land from the government.

The first purchase under the authority of this act was the 81,303 acre estate of Charles Worrell for £24,000 in late 1854. Even this purchase was fraught with corruption. William Henry Pope who was acting for Worrell deceived him on the value of the property and bought it for £14,000, thus Pope stood to receive a quick £10,000 to line his own pocket. As it was, Pope only received £7,000 because he did not transfer all of the estate and the government withheld the other £3,000. The other major estate bought in the 1850's was the Selkirk estate, purchased in 1859.

All of this land was located in the Liberated Area. Although the Escheat Party had been unable to enforce Escheat, it was their militancy which persuaded the landlords in this area to sell when they had the chance since the tenants refused to pay rent anyway. The majority of the land held by landlords in other parts of the Island remained in their hands until the compulsory Land Purchase Act was passed in 1875.

In 1854, the Liberal Party split over the question of salaries of government officials. While they quarrelled among themselves the Conservatives won the election.

The Conservatives attempted to remove government officials from direct responsibility to the Assembly by advocating that they be appointed from outside the elected assembly—a sort of semi-permanent civil service to which the Compact would be able to appoint their supporters. This was directly contrary to the concept and practice of responsible government.

Outraged at this obstruction, Lt.-Governor Bannerman used his power to dissolve the Assembly. Coles and the Liberals had regrouped and were returned to power just six months after being defeated.

Religion brought into the Fray

Religion was always a contentious issue in the British Empire. In England the bourgois revolution was carried out by Protestants and many of the conquered people of the British Isles, particularly Ireland, were Catholic. The Catholic religion was repressed by the protestants who not only ran the government but owned most of the industry and large properties. In Britain and in the colonies, Catholics did not have a vote until the 1830's and '40's. In the colonies, many of the immigrants were Catholics who had left the British Isles in an attempt to escape persecution. Here the English held firmly to a policy of promoting and advancing the Protestant churches with special land grants, political influence, etc. Catholics were kept out of government and as much as possible attempts were made to integrate them into a Protestant dominated community. In P.E.I. this was made more difficult because of the radicalizing effect of the land struggle. A large number of the tenants were Catholics who had fought for Escheat, a fight which on occasion broke out into open battles as in the case of the Belfast riot. In the 1850's the ratio between Protestants and Catholics on the Island was 55-45.

Religions on P.E.I		
Anglican	6,785	
Church of Scotland	10,271	
Presbyterians	15,591	
Methodist	5,809	
Other Protestant	6,340	
Total Protestant		44,796
Catholics		35,852
Total Population		80,648

In 1852, the government of George Coles introduced the Free

Education Act. It established a school system which provided free elementary education to all Islanders. Prior to this Act, pupils' fees provided the greater part of the money needed to run the schools and pay the teachers' salaries. Under the new Act, school districts, each with a Board of Trustees to administer the affairs of the schools, were established. A district board was responsible for the upkeep of its school and for part of the teacher's salary; the balance came from the colonial government.

One of the provisions of the Act limited the use of the Bible in schools to "reading without interpretation", and then only at the request of a majority of the parents.

However, the Protestants were dissatisfied and demanded Bible interpretation, *their* interpretation, in the public schools. The question flared into open controversy in 1856 when, at the opening of the new Normal School, built to train teachers for the expanding school population, the principal, John Stark, stated that the classes each day would open and close with prayer and Bible reading "in which the true facts of Scripture will be brought before the children's mind by illustrations and picture words, in language simple and easy to understand."[1]

The Catholic clergy, led by the Bishop of Charlottetown, Bernard MacDonald, saw this as a move by the Protestants, particularly the Anglicans, to wipe out the Catholic religion. He wrote a letter to George Coles and the Board of Education asking that the provisions of the 1852 education act be upheld. Coles explained to the Bishop that no change in the school system was intended and that Stark's comments were made on his own without the authority of the Board of Education.

But Stark had given the Protestants the opening they wanted and they were quick to take advantage of it. Rev. David Fitzgerald, an Anglican clergyman in Charlottetown and a member of the Board of Education, contended that "Roman interests were ascending in Prince Edward Island."[2] Determined to see the use of the Bible in public schools he asserted that "no earthly consideration will induce us to submit to any attempt to deprive us of our rights and privileges as subjects of the British Crown."[3]

A meeting of Protestants was held in Charlottetown on Friday,

February 13, 1857. It was attended by Col. John Hamilton Grey, a Conservative, who expressed "a deep sense of service to Rev. David Fitzgerald and Mr. Stark in bringing under the notice of Protestants of this Island the letter of the Roman Catholic Bishop of Charlottetown." He further said that "had they not acted so, this meeting is of the opinion that they would have been guilty of a betrayal of Protestant interests."[4]

However, Conservatives like Grey and Fitzgerald were interested in politics, not religion. The Conservatives knew that they could not defeat the Liberals in an election unless they could find some controversial issue to divide the electorate in their favor. The religious controversy was perfect.

In the 1859 election campaign they came out in favor of Bible interpretation. Another leading Conservative, W. H. Pope, a declared atheist, fanned the flames of antagonism by writing letters to Island Protestants damning the Catholic religion. Pope was a petty, bigoted opportunist who spread vicious lies and rumours. In one letter he wrote "a Catholic woman going to confess to a priest is the same as taking a mare to a stallion."[5]

In the 1858 election the Liberals won by a margin of two seats. They lost seats because of the religious issue and also because the tenants were dissatisfied with the slow pace of the land purchase programme. When one member resigned, Coles had no choice but to ask for a new election.

In the election of 1859, the Conservatives, supported by the Protestants, won on strict religious grounds by a margin of 19-11.

The Conservatives then moved to make the Legislative Council (the upper house) an elected body because the majority of the appointees were Liberals. Lt.-Governor Dundas in a letter to the Colonial Office wrote that the Conservatives "represent the educated and respectable classes" and the Liberals "as obscure, ineducated and ignorant, selected from the lower classes."[6] He recommended that he be allowed to appoint five more members to the Legislative Council so that the Conservatives would have a majority in that body. This was agreed to and the Colonial Office was saved from the possibility of having an elected upper house— a very un-British practice.

The question of interpretation was settled in 1860 when the same Conservatives who had stirred up the controversy over religious education upheld the 1852 Education Act.

In 1863, the Liberal Party gave support to St. Dunstan's Roman Catholic College in its request for some government funding. The Conservatives refused the request. They took advantage of the rekindled flames of religious controversy and won the election held that year.

But 45% of the population could not be ignored. When the Conservatives passed a bill to incorporate the Orange Lodge, a Protestant organisation with the expressed aim of doing everything possible to destroy Catholicism, Catholics on the Island were outraged. They sent a petition with 11,000 signatures to the Imperial government demanding that the bill be disallowed. The Imperial government complied rather than face civil war in the colony.

Chapter Notes

1. quoted in MacKinnon, Wayne E., *The Life of the Party; A History of the Liberal Party of Prince Edward Island*, Charlottetown, 1973, p. 29.
2. *Ibid*, p. 31.
3. *Ibid.*, p. 31.
4. *Ibid*, p. 31.
5. Ian Ross Robertson, "William Henry Pope" in Marc La Terreur, *Directory of Canadian Biography, Vol. X, 1871-1880*. Toronto, U of T Press, 1972.
6. PAC., M.G. 11, C.O. 226 "Dundas—Newcastle", October 17, 1859.

14

Warfare
in the country

Social and Political Structures

Perhaps the most significant result of the colony's hard-fought
progress towards self-government was the enactment and imple-
mentation of the land purchase act. Nevertheless, as long as the
Imperial government in London saw as its principal and ultimate
purpose the protection of the interests of the Island's major landowners and chief merchants, democratic self-government was far
from complete.

The tenants and small farmers had given their support to the
Liberal governments of George Coles but they still relied for their
greatest security on their ability to ward off the sheriff and rent
collectors. In the Liberated Area, few rents had been paid since
the '30's.

In the 1850's and 1860's, the tenant farmers began to arm
themselves. This they did by joining the militia and then desert-
ing, taking their muskets with them. Reports such as the following sent in November 1859 accompanied almost every ship
headed for England. "When the sheriff went to the St Mary's
Road settlement, (to collect rent arrears) 10 miles from Georgetown, his horse was shot and a group of men drove him off with
musket shot.

"The sheriff then collected 25 muskets in Charlottetown and
proceeded to raise by summons 25 or 30 constables but on two

occasions once in St Mary's and once in Georgetown was unable to get men to go with him as constables.''[1]

The solidarity of the tenants against their oppressors drove a wedge between the countryside and the city, the headquarters of the tenants and landlords respectively.

My Rural Home

O tell me of the city gay,
Or towns where merchants be,
Where the luxury riots from day to day.
In the haunts of rivalry.

Though they be haunts of fashion or wealth
They're also the haunts of sin,
And not conclusive to vigorous health
And happiness felt within.[2]

The Land Commission

In 1860 the Imperial government appointed a land commission to investigate, report and make recommendations to solve the land struggles. It consisted of Joseph Howe, leader of Nova Scotia's fight for responsible government, representing the Island Assembly, John H. Gray, from St. John, New Brunswick representing the Imperial government and J. W. Ritchie, a Halifax lawyer, representing the landlords.

The commissioners' report, submitted in 1861, opposed escheat on the grounds that the land titles had been held too long. It proposed: (a) that the Imperial government guarantee a loan of £100,000 to buy out the landlords; (b) that if this were not accepted tenants be allowed to buy land they tilled from the landlords; (c) that fishery reserves be abolished and that those wishing to establish fisheries be given one acre of land adjacent; (d) that loyalists who could prove claims be given Crown lands; (e) that the claims of Acadien settlers for land be rejected on the grounds that they were the victims of history, and (f) that the native people be granted Lennox Island as a permanent reserve. [3]

The recommendations were approved by the Assembly but were rejected by the Imperial government. The rejection by London of a report approved by the Assembly of the people directly affected by the report served but to confirm that "responsible self-government" in a colony is a mere pretence and a distortion of truth.

The Island Tenants' League

The reaction of the tenants was swift and militant. For the first time they were organised on an Island-wide basis and in 1864, the Island Tenants' League was formed. Its purpose was to withhold all rent until the landlords agreed to sell land on terms considered just by the League.

By now every tenant knew that when he heard the sound of the tin horn or the conch shell it would be a summons to stand with his neighbours in defence of his land against the approaching sheriff and constables.

On March 17, 1865, the tenants crossed the ice from Southport to march on the Colonial Building where the legislature was in session, under the direction of the party in power—their old enemies the Conservatives. They carried signs and banners demanding *Free Land* and *Tenants' Rights*. Together they directed almost a hundred years of anger and frustration at the Colonial compradors.

When one of their number, Samuel Fletcher, of Alberry Plains, was arrested they tore down the sheriff's office where he was being held and freed him.

On March 22 the governor issued a proclamation declaring the Tenants' League an unlawful association and the government took action against Fletcher.

On April 7, a force of 200 men was assembled to go to Alberry Plains to arrest him. The force was composed mostly of citizens of Charlottetown, many of whom were sympathetic to the tenants. The cavalry, composed of landlords' agents and friends, went ahead. The infantry, most of them tenant sympathizers, took up the rear. While the Cavalry forged ahead, the infantry made all manner of excuses to lag behind. At 10 a.m. they stopped 4 miles from Charlottetown to have tea at a place called today Tea Hill. By this time the cavalry was closing in on Vernon River, 10 miles ahead, where they were faced by a "battery of cannon manned" by Tenant Leaguers.

The mounted men advanced under a flag of truce only to find that the "fort" consisted of nothing more than a few pieces of old stove pipe thrust through a board with a number of hats stuck on top to represent men. The hatless Tenant Leaguers watched in amusement from a nearby woods.

Undaunted, though embarrassed, the Cavalry continued their advance. When they got to Fletcher's farm, they saw him standing by his gate and charged forward to make their capture—of a straw-filled effigy of Fletcher!

Completely embarrassed they marched back toward Charlottetown rejoining the infantry but a few miles from Tea Hill. As evening fell they rode into the city beaten by a straw man and stove pipes to face a taunting public.

Following this humiliation, the government passed the Freehold Purchase Act which provided loans to tenants of up to half the cost of land purchase. But the tenants were not pacified. They continued to defend their land and increase their guerilla activities.

On May 27, the landlord of lot 36 successfully served writs on his tenants. A few days later his barns burned down and the government, to no avail, offered a reward of £500.

In July the sheriff was intercepted 10 miles from Charlottetown where he and the bailiff were attacked by tenants. Writs of possession were seized and torn up. One tenant, Charles Dickenson, was arrested and jailed in Charlottetown. On the day of his trial, 1000 tenants entered the city to protest. The Colonial Secretary was forced to place armed guards at the armories, the gun powder magazine and the jail. Dickinson was never convicted because, as was by now a common occurrence, a jury of his peers could not be found that would convict him.

Following this series of attacks, the sheriff, Thomas A. Todd, in a letter to the new Colonial Secretary wrote: "I am completely powerless to execute any writs placed in my hands. This case is one of such a serious nature that no time ought to be lost in taking the military into your serious consideration."[4]

In July, the government, through the Board of Education, took action against school teachers who supported the League. The support among teachers was widespread as all rural residents united against the Compact forces.

Board of Education Notice[5]

Extract from the minutes of the Board of Education, at the monthly meeting held on the 27th of July, 1865, viz:

The Board having received information that several teachers holding licences from this Board, and in receipt of salaries from the public funds, have absented themselves from their schools, and have attended and taken part in the meetings of a certain Association denounced as unlawful, in the Proclamation of His Excellency the Lieutenant Governor, dated the 22nd day of March last—the Board orders public notice to be given that every teacher, so offending in the future, shall be struck off the role of licensed teachers, and payment of his salary stopped forthwith.

By order of the Board
   John McNeill, Secretary

In early August, a Tenants' League meeting in lot 31, west of Charlottetown, adopted two resolutions:

Resolved that the repeated failure of successive governments to settle the land question prove that they are either unable or unwilling to do so and that it now becomes the duty of the people to do for themselves what their representatives in parliament have failed to effect. Moved Will Clark, Seconded Richard Bowman.

Resolved that it is our duty to unite as tenants, for mutual protection and sympathy in order to put an end to the leasehold system by offering to purchase in accordance with the report of the Land Commission and the action of our legislature. Moved Charles Kitson, Seconded Tom Godfrey.[6]

Confrontations between sheriffs and tenants took place every time an attempt was made to collect rents or issue writs. The following account of an early morning raid by the Queen's County sheriff is typical of the state of rebellion which existed. It is a description of the arrest of Fabian Doucette on the morning of August 10, 1865:

We arrived at Doucette's shortly after daybreak this morning, and proceeded cautiously to his house.

Although men had been stationed by Doucette in his out-houses . . . it seemed upon this occasion they had gone to sleep at their post, and we were thus enabled to surround the house before we were discovered.

The moment we were discovered the men in the outhouses immediately began to blow their trumpets and although we silenced them as soon as we possibly could, but it was not before this signal had been heard and answered from farm to farm.

We at once turned our attention to the dwelling house, through the windows of which we saw the man against whom I held the warrant. As they refused us entrance I ordered the door to be broken open and when we entered we found that Doucette had retreated upstairs and with a number of men armed with large sticks prevented us getting after him.

Several times the attempt was made by my men but the opening of the stairs was so narrow that they were unable to defend themselves and from the heavy and repeated blows showered upon them, were knocked down several times and received severe bruises.

I then ordered an entrance to be made through an end window but as soon as it had been forced open and one of my men was in the act of entering he received a severe blow on the head which felled him to the ground.

During this time trumpets were blown by some of Doucette's accomplices and were answered from farm to farm and I feared that such a number of men would soon collect as could rescue Doucette even if we succeeded in taking him.

We at last succeeded in forcing our way partly upstairs but not before all my men had been struck and some of them severely bruised, one of them seized Doucette by the hair of his head and dragged him down and we secured him.

Owing to the number of men we saw collecting I did not think it judicious to endeavour to make any other prisoners, and the information I subsequently received confirms the opinion I then formed, for we had not left the place more than a few minutes before (I have been since informed) a hundred men had collected for the purpose of rescuing any prisoners we arrested or property we had levied upon . . . [7]

In the same letter the sheriff said that "their system of terrorism is such that the sheriff can look for no assistance outside of the towns."[8] He concluded that he felt that the only reason Doucette was captured was because he and his men had firearms.

The sheriff again pleaded with Pope to send for a military force saying that "the force at my command is inadequate" to issue writs or make arrests.

Both the Liberals and the Conservatives were in panic. Both agreed that the troops must be called to preserve the peace. Faced with the threat of direct attack by the tenants, the compradors and the Island bourgeoisie united to oppose this organised militancy. For both these classes, power in the hands of the people had to be stopped at all costs. A few days later 140 British troops from the garrison in Halifax arrived on Prince Edward Island.

The tenants continued to fight. On September 18, the sheriff and his men were hemmed in on the Rocky Point wharf by a large body of men and were so terrified that they fled by boat across the harbour to Charlottetown.

The soldiers were well armed with up-to-date British firearms. The tenants could not match their fire power and so resorted to harassing tactics to slow them down.

Soon after the military arrived, George Adams, the president of the Tenants' League deserted and left his friends to fend for themselves. Against the advancing military and without a leader the tenants resorted to burning the bridges and obstructing the roads. By late October the military was able to issue writs in lots 22 and 65. In late November soldiers were dispatched to lots 35 and 36 in the Tracadie area north of Charlottetown and to lots 48, 49 and 50 to the east.

By the end of the year the tenants had been subdued and the troops were sent back to Halifax. The compradors allied with the Island bourgeoisie had won a victory but no government could be assured of peace until the last landlord had left the colony. The land question became an important factor in the Confederation discussions which commenced in 1864.

Chapter Notes

1. PAC., M.G. 11, C.O. 226, "Dundas to Newcastle", November 28, 1859.
2. *Charlottetown Patriot*, September 5, 1868, author unknown.
3. "Land Commission Report", *P.E.I. Assembly Journals*, Appendix E, Public Archives, Charlottetown.
4. "Thos. A. Todd to W.H. Pope", July 19, 1865, Public Archives, P.E.I.
5. Public Archives, P.E.I.
6. PAC., M.G. 11, C.O. 226, "Hodgson to Cardwell", August 16, 1865.
7. PAC., M.G. 11, C.O. 226, "Sheriff of Queen's to W.H. Pope", enclosed in "Hodgson to Cardwell", August 16, 1865.
8. Ibid.

15

Confederation

The Golden Age

The two decades between 1850 and 1870 were the golden age of the Maritime Colonies. The British Empire had become a great empire of trade and commerce. The fine sailing ships which carried the trade were built in these colonies and from Maritime ports sailed the seven seas. It was a time of prosperity and the three Maritime colonies, as important parts of the British imperial power, shared in it.

In 1855 a reciprocity treaty was signed between Britain and the United States. Foodstuffs and materials were allowed to be traded freely between the United States and the British Colonies in North America. In Prince Edward Island the illegal trade carried on between the tenant farmers and United States' fishermen became lawful. Between 1845 and 1865 the Island's legal trade increased fourfold. In 1865, the United States supplied 24% of the Islands imports and received 42.2% of its exports.

Reciprocity brought a great demand for agricultural products. The purchase of some of the larger estates, Worrell's and Selkirk's in the 1850's and the 200,000-acre Cunard estate in 1866, encouraged the new freeholder owners to work hard to meet the increased demand. Agriculture flourished. For the first time indigenous, independent Island merchants handled the trade. After years of economic stagnation the Island prospered. In 1860 the editor of the *Islander* wrote:

> There are but few men possessed of great wealth in the
> country but there are thousands who commenced the world
> without a pound, who, by farming alone, have acquired
> valuable properties—rendered themselves independent—
> and have been able to give their sons good farms—and there
> is not to be found an instance of a well conducted, industri-
> ous and sober man failing to make a comfortable living. [1]

Yet large tracts of land still remained in the hands of absentee
landlords and the leasehold tenure system remained the biggest
block to progress. It was this land tenure system that caused the
1865 tenants' uprisings.

Island Imports and Exports to the U.S.A. (official) [2]		
	Imports	**Exports**
1844	1.5%	2.4%
1850	7.5%	17.0%
1855	16.0%	22.0%
1860	25.0%	38.5%
1865	24.0%	42.2%
1865*	17.0%	9.0%
*the year following the end of Reciprocity		

The Confederation Debates

In the years leading up to Confederation, the Island's economy
continued to depend upon agriculture and shipping. But the
merchant bourgeoisie of Canada were ushering in the railway age
of steel and steam. The merchants, who of course dominated the
Canadian provincial legislature, were voting themselves huge
sums of public money to finance their ventures and granting to
the chartered railway companies, of which they were the principal
shareholders, vast blocks of crown land.

In Nova Scotia and New Brunswick there were merchants who
could see the immense fortunes to be made from opening up the
railways and these men seized the opportunities to join in the
ventures. Led by Charles Tupper in Nova Scotia and by Leonard
Tilly in New Brunswick, these maritime merchants joined with
the political leaders of Canada, John A. Macdonald of Upper

Canada and Georges E. Cartier of Lower Canada, to discuss a political union of the British north American colonies. Such a union, they calculated, would be to their economic advantage. (No doubt, like a president of General Motors many decades later, they argued that what was good for their businesses was good for their countries.)

The two larger Maritime colonies started promoting a conference on Maritime union in 1863. The Canadas, eager to present their own plans for the larger union, took an immediate interest.

The Island government was not interested in union. The merchants in Charlottetown controlled a solid, if small, merchant trade and wanted no part of any union which might threaten their small empire. However, after prodding from Tupper and Tilly, the Island government decided that it would do no harm to "sit down and have a discussion," if the conference was held in Charlottetown. The other two maritime colonies, with much more to gain from economic union because of their greater trade and their year-round access to the sea, conceded this request. The conference was set for September 1, 1864 in the Island capital.

The government of the colony of Canada wanted to take part in the conference. Sir John A. Macdonald, the Prime Minister of the Canadian parliament, wrote to George Dundas, the Lt. Governor of P.E.I, requesting permission for a delegation to come to the conference "as observers". Dundas dutifully responded by issuing an invitation.

The enthusiasm of the Island government for the conference was hardly overwhelming. When the delegates from the other colonies arrived not a single member of the government showed up in an official capacity to meet them; they were all attending a circus which was visiting the city. Nevertheless the conference started as planned on the afternoon of Thursday, September 1. After a few hours of discussion among the Maritime delegates the floor was taken by the Canadian delegates who proposed their scheme for union. Canada's proposal, along with a plan to make available £200,000 to buy out the landlords, was welcomed by the Island delegates who were quick to see the benefits. It, they thought, offered them a way to end the leasehold tenure system, to be a part of a larger union and yet to retain their own government and control over their merchant interests.

The birth of Canada was proclaimed unofficially on the deck of the Upper Canadian ship *Queen Victoria* on Saturday evening, September 3, 1864, when the bourgeois politicians under the influence of good food and liquor got carried away. Many heated debates were to follow before the proclamation became official.

Delegates to the Confederation Conferences
C — Charlottetown   Q — Québec

P.E.I.		New Brunswick (cont'd.)	
John H. Gray	C, Q	W.H. Shevies	C, Q
Edward Palmer	C, Q	C. Fisher	Q
W.H. Pope	C, Q	P. Mitchell	Q
George Coles	C, Q		
A.A. MacDonald	C, Q	Canada	
T.H. Haviland	Q	John A. Macdonald	C, Q
Edward Whelan	Q	George E. Cartier	C, Q
H. Bernard	Q	Alexander Galt	C, Q
		George Brown	C, Q
Nova Scotia		William McDougal	C, Q
Charles Tupper	C, Q	Thomas D'Arcy McGee	C, Q
William A. Henry	C, Q	Hector Longevin	C, Q
Robert B. Dickey	C, Q	Alexander Campbell	C, Q
Jonathan McWilly	C, Q	Sir E.P. Tache	C, Q
Adams C. Archibald	C, Q	O. Howatt	Q
		J.C. Chapais	Q
New Brunswick		J. Cockburn	Q
S.L. Tilley	C, Q		
J.M. Johnson	C, Q	Newfoundland	
J.H. Gray	C, Q	F.B.T. Charter	Q
Edeard B. Chandler	C, Q	J.A. Shea	Q

In the nine days the delegates were in Charlottetown, formal meetings took only 22 hours. The rest of the time was spent at a series of parties and dinners which offered the Canadian delegates ample opportunity to woo their Maritime colleagues. On September 10, the conference adjourned to Halifax where, after more wining and dining, it was decided to hold an official Confederation Conference in Québec City on October 11.

At the Québec Conference, Island delegate Edward Whelan, a

Charlottetown: *An aerial view of the city from the harbour looking north east. The large buildings in the centre of the picture are on the site of the present day confederation centre. The building on the right with the pillars is the legislature building which still stands. (PAC).*

Shoreline: *While there are many sandy beaches all along the shore, there are also sandstone cliffs like this one which rise as much as forty feet out of the water. (PAPEI).*

Liberal, joined Conservatives John Hamilton Gray, Pope and Haviland to give hesitant support to Confederation; while Palmer, a Conservative, joined Liberals MacDonald and Coles to oppose it. Throughout the conference the two groups argued with each other. They united only when the financial arrangements for Confederation were discussed. When it bcame clear that the money to buy out the landlords was not to be part of the agreement, only the staunchest supporters of the scheme, Whelan, Gray and Haviland continued to support it.

When the delegates returned to the Island, they found outright opposition to the Confederation plan. The tenants saw no advantage in joining a union to remain under the tutelage of British landlords. Freehold farmers and workers who had fought against British imperialism, were reaping the benefits of expanded trade and wanted no part of a union with the Canadas.

The bourgeoisie was split. Small manufacturers like Coles had built up flourishing businesses in the colony. They saw only increased competition at best and outright bankruptcy at worst as the centralised economy proposed by the union wiped out their small enterprises. Political-military careerist John Hamilton Gray and journalist Edward Whelan saw that the larger union would be to their advantage. W.H. Pope spoke for a group of wholesale merchants who stood to gain with a greater volume of imported manufactured goods from central Canada under Confederation.

There was also opposition to the union in Nova Scotia and New Brunswick from merchants who had made their fortunes in lumbering, fishing and shipbuilding. Like their counterparts on the Island they wanted to preserve their position. However, after a two-year struggle the powerful railway interests, led by Tupper and Tilly, carried the Confederation resolutions through the legislatures at Halifax and Fredericton. In fact the Confederation resolution was defeated in New Brunswick in 1865 and only narrowly passed in time for the representation to London in 1867.

When the debate opened in the Island legislature the Conservative government was torn with dissension. The pro-Confederate group advocated union until it was clear no amount of persuassion was going to change the minds of the overwhelming majority of the legislators or the people. They then changed their tactics—speaking publicly against union or saying nothing, while secretly working to bring it about.

The tenant uprising of 1865 strengthened the arguments of the anti-Confederates. The Confederation scheme offered no solution to the biggest problem on the Island—the leasehold tenure system. When the vote finally came in the legislature the scheme for union was defeated by a resounding 23 to 5.

In spite of the defeat the pro-Confederates did not give up. In 1867, J.C. Pope, in London at the time of the presentation of the B.N.A. Act to the British Parliament, met with and suggested to Tilly that if the Dominion were to offer the Island a grant of $800,000 to buy out the landlords, Confederation might be possible. The offer was made and although Pope's judgement, on this occasion, was wrong, he did not relent.

While the pro-Confederation faction schemed, the British and Canadian governments were concerned and worried about the outcome. Although the Island had little to offer economically, it was feared that as a separate colony it would become a meeting place for smugglers to move goods into Canada. This fear was heightened when the group opposed to Confederation started agitating for a separate Reciprocity Treaty with the United States. Island merchants had suffered a great loss in 1865 when the treaty was rescinded and their export trade decreased by 38%.

Effect of Reciprocity Withdrawal[3]		
Product	Quantity Exported to the U.S. 1865	Quantity Exported to the U.S. 1866
Oats	705,570 Bushels	nil
Barley	42,415 Bushels	nil
Potatoes	114,277 Bushels	75 Bushels
Butter	20,960 Pounds	730 Pounds
Eggs	1,550 Barrels	907 Barrels
Mackerel	116,530 Barrels	13,488 Barrels

Total value 1865 £120,928
Total value 1866 £ 21,633

In 1868, the Island government, without consulting Britain,

initiated negotiations with the United States and a delegation from Washington visited Charlottetown to discuss reciprocity. When the Imperial government heard of this "impudent" act, government officials on the Island were ordered promptly to cease their discussions with the Americans. The Colonial Office also took other measures to put pressure on the colony. The Island government was ordered to pay the Lieutenant-Governor's salary. Marine regulations, that in Canada had been legislated by the parliament, were imposed by London and a request for a loan to buy out the landlords was turned down. In an attempt to deal with this vital issue of land ownership, the colony's government introduced legislation which would require the landlords to sell. The imperial government vetoed the passage of the bill. Yet even these acts of imperial arrogance were insufficient to bend the will of the people regarding Confederation. What they did was to stiffen anti-British sentiment.

Land Distribution 1868[4]		
Freehold		450,000 acres
Owned by Government		244,799 "
Leased	209,712 acres	
Unsettled	459,888 "	
Owned by Landlords		669,600 acres
Total Land		1,365,400 "

One farmer when asked about loyalty to Britain said that some claimed that there is evidence for such loyalty but "It is no sign of a duck's nest to find a feather on a stone." Two papers on the Island, *The North Star*, published in Charlottetown, and the *Summerside Progress* openly advocated annexation to the United States. Even pro-Confederate, Edward Whelan, had no love for Britain. In his paper, *The Examiner*, he wrote "talk about the glorious privileges of the British constitution; we live under a constitution of dispatches dictated according to the caprice of the absentee landlords."[5]

Despite their resentment against Britain the annexationists offered no better solution. A look at the State of Maine today is sufficient to show what could have been in store for the Island had it become an offshore island outpost of the United States.

Throughout this time, the pro-Confederates were carrying on a continuous correspondence with John A. Macdonald advising him on the situation.

A letter from Macdonald to C.W. DeBlois, February 1870, reveals the plot.

> I have to thank you very much for your interesting letter ... and am glad to hear that the prospects of Confederation in your Island are, though perhaps slowly, certainly brightening ...
>
> The rising generation in Prince Edward Island is particularly interested it seems to me, in the scheme. It opens a wide field for their industry, experience and ambition, without expropriation or change of allegiance. Your judges will be better paid, your legal men will have a larger field for their talent, and most classes of your population will gain and none that I can see, can possibly lose by the union.
>
> With respect to your agricultural production, you have been hitherto put on the same footing as if you were already a part of the Dominion. I shall be sorry to see this changed, but if you will persist in holding aloof from Canada and treating us as a foreign country, you must not be surprised if some day the Canadian Parliament shall treat the Island in the same fashion.
>
> I shall be extremely obliged by hearing from you from time to time when your leisure will permit as to the state of the question on the Island.
>
> Believe me,
> Yours Faithfully,
> (Signed) John A. Macdonald[6]

The Railway Brings Confederation

In 1871, the pro-Confederates pulled their ace out of their sleeve. They convinced the merchants that the Island needed a railway, and a bill to authorise the building of a railway from Tignish to Souris was passed in the legislature. It was proposed that the money to build the railway be raised by selling Island notes to London bankers.

Lt.-Governor Robinson was pleased about the passing of the railway bill, for, as he informed the Colonial Office, " ... it will eventually mean that P.E.I. will join Confederation."[7]

The people were alarmed. A letter to the *Charlottetown Examiner* reporting on a visit to an Island farmer reveals the apprehension. The writer says:

> He invited me in, and the first words he said were "Well friend are they going on with the railway?" "Yes, I believe they are." "Oh! They'll ruin the country. It's a scheme by the Popes to get us into Confederation ..."[8]

Railway construction began and the government incurred a large debt. When Charles Palmer, President of the Union Bank, went to London to sell Island bonds, he was told by London bankers that they would buy the notes if they were assured that the Island would enter Confederation.

The farmer was right. In 1873, the Island was faced with an enormous debt for railway construction and the work was far from complete. Because the Island had accumulated no debt until railway building began there is little doubt that it could have absorbed the cost and eventually finished the railway. But the pro-Confederates insisted that the only way out was to join Confederation. They negotiated with the Canadian Cabinet and an agreement was reached. The Canadian government was to provide an $800,000 loan to buy out the remaining landlords, assume the railway debt and finish the project. The people accepted this rather than the debt and on July 1, 1873, the Island became a province of Canada.

In 1875, the federal parliament passed the Land Purchase Act. Under the Act, absentee landlords and large resident landlords were forced to sell their land to the Island government at a price set by the Act.

Chapter Notes

1. *The Islander*, Charlottetown, January 13, 1860.
2. PAC., M.G. 11, C.O. 226, "Statistics on Exports and Imports with the United States, 1840-1867", transmitted August, 1869.
3. PAC., M.G. 11, C.O. 226, "Effect of Reciprocity Withdrawal" in "Dundas to Buckingham, February 7, 1868.
4. PAC., M.G. 11, C.O. 226, "Blue Book Report for 1870", transmitted February, 1872.
5. *The Examiner* in David Weale, "Prince Edward Island and Confederation Debates", M.A. Thesis, Queen's University, 1971.
6. In *Charlottetown Patriot*, July 14, 1939, "John A. Macdonald to C.W. DeBlois Esq.," February 9, 1870. Public Archives, P.E.I.
7. PAC., M.G. 11, C.O. 226, "Robinson to Kimberley", April 17, 1871.
8. *The Examiner*, April 24, 1871.

Processing Fish: *Above, here the fish are being washed and salted and, below, being laid out to dry in the sun. (PAC).*

16

Resource hinterland for imperialism

The Bourgeois Dream is Shattered

From the days of the first settlements until the time of Confederation, the people of Prince Edward Island had been largely self-sufficient. They cultivated the land and fished the seas. Most of what they needed was made by skilled craftsmen in small workshops on the Island. Their external trade was with Britain, the United States, the West Indies, Newfoundland and the other Maritime colonies.

Confederation and the setting up of the National Policy* brought great changes. In Ottawa's scheme of things, the Island became a hinterland of central Canada from which the natural and agricultural resources were extracted and to which the manufactured products of central Canada were sold under the protection of a tariff. The manufacturers of central Canada were the ones to be protected; the Islanders were the losers. Their trade with their traditional suppliers and markets declined or was subject to control by Ottawa, their small manufacturing workshops were unable to compete with the factories of Upper Canada and their wooden-ship building industry was reduced to the point of extinction.

*The National Policy set up tariff barriers to protect the manufacturing of central Canada. It however did not protect the Island manufacturers who lost their business to the larger factories in Upper Canada.

The Railway

Before the advent of the railway, land transportation was extremely difficult. Roads were so poor they were often unusable. Agricultural produce for export would be taken by the shortest route to one of the ports which were to be found in virtually every bay around the coast. In these ports flourishing shipbuilding yards employed hundreds of workers. For thirty years before Confederation these ports and their shipbuilding activities were crucial to the Island's expanding import-export trade.

Two events, the building of the railway and the introduction of steamships into the waters around the Island brought drastic changes to the life of the Island communities. With the coming of steam and steel, the Island's shipbuilding industry collapsed, the lumbering industry fell into a decline from which it never recovered, the once busy ports lost their trade and their industry and, most significantly a new class of comprador middlemen replaced the landlords and the Family Compact in controlling the Island's government.

Shipbuilding—Rise and Fall [1]					
Year	No. Ships	Tonnage	Year	No. Ships	Tonnage
1846	84	12,283	1865	126	34,286
1850	93	14,367	1866	127	31,932
1854	106	24,111	1868	75	18,666
1858	69	13,073	1872	60	13,172
1862	80	18,418	1882	14	3,776
1863	110	24,991	1890	10	1,499
1864	119	33,330			

By the time the railway had been built from Tignish in the north west to Souris in the east, farm produce was being hauled from stations located every three miles or so along the line between the two chief ports of Charlottetown and Summerside. Merchants in these two ports were handling close to ninety percent of the railborne commerce, three quarters of it in Charlottetown. Most of this trade was being handled by companies like R.T. Holman, Ltd., Carvell Bros. Ltd., and Prowse Bros. Ltd., each of which had its own private wharves; Holman's in Summerside, the latter two in Charlottetown.

When the railway became the main carrier of Island commerce and the smaller ports fell into decay, the majority of Islanders, who lived on and tilled the land, turned their eyes from the sea to the land, from Britain to Canada.

The End of Feudalism

Under the terms of Confederation, the Island government was given a loan of $800,000 to purchase the remaining land held by landlords. The Land Purchase Act of 1875 made it compulsory for the remaining landlords to sell at a price determined by the commission appointed under the Act.

For $1.63 an acre, the provincial government bought a little under half of the 382,000 acres of land still in the hands of the landlords. This was done within one year of the passing of the act. The remaining properties were bought only after the owners, led by R.D. Stewart, who held over 67,000 acres, were defeated in extended court battles. The last case was settled in the Supreme Court of Canada in 1895, twenty years after the Act became law. In all, the Island government borrowed $782,400 to buy back the land. Resident farmers were given the first option to buy from the government. The loan has never been repaid to the federal government and the interest each year is deducted from the federal grants to the Island government.

In the forty years that elapsed between the purchase of the Worrell estate in 1854 until the final purchase in 1895, an ever increasing number of farmers became owners of the property on which they laboured. This change in ownership was reflected in increased productivity; most noticeably in the dairy sector and particularly in the final decade of the century. Butter production increased from 16,040 lbs. in 1890 to 1,840,245 lbs. in 1900; cheese production from 811,650 lbs. to 6,918,352 lbs. To handle the increased production, butter and cheese factories were built in many of the small communities served by the railway.

The Growth of the Fishing Industry

The 1860's also brought rapid growth in the fishing industry. After the Reciprocity Treaty ended in 1865, United States fishermen left the coastal waters and Islanders for the first time fished in large numbers. Between 1870 and 1880, the number employed in fishing and related industry more than tripled from 1,646 to 5,792, and the number of fishing vessels more than doubled from 1,183 to 2,729. Fish processing plants developed as an important secondary industry employing many men left unemployed when the shipbuilding industry declined.

For a time this increased production brought prosperity to the Island. It also strengthened the merchants who handled the trade in Summerside and Charlottetown. The long established trading patterns set up before Confederation absorbed the increased production for a few years with little being sent to the provinces in Upper Canada.

The Decline of Manufacturing

However, it was not long before Confederation and the consequent National Policy started to have an impact.

Just as the building of the Island railway centralised and concentrated the economy of the Island in the ports of Charlottetown and Summerside, the building of the railway in the rest of Canada centralised and concentrated the industry and economy of the whole country in a narrow strip along the St. Lawrence river between Montreal and Hamilton. The Branch lines extended east, west and north to bring the resources of these regions into this industrial heartland.

The federal government's National Policy of import tariffs protected the new industries of the Canadian heartland from unwanted competition, particularly from the U.S. For the existing and potential secondary industries of other parts of the nation, the National Policy had a devastating effect. Outside southern Ontario the regional economies came under the control of a small comprador class of middlemen through whose businesses natural resources flowed to the centre and manufactured goods were sold to the people of the Canadian hinterland. For the farmers and the workers, little had changed.

In P.E.I., the small local industries including manufacturers of leather, boots and shoes, farm machinery, clothing, furniture, etc., which had developed to supply the needs of the growing population, were protected by a local tariff before Confederation. The removal of these tariffs after Confederation and the inflow of goods mass produced in central Canada spelled doom for these small industrial concerns.

Employment Tables[2]		
	1881	1891
Carpenters	1,094	1,102
*Apparel Makers	1,079	1,074
*Mariners	765	539
*Blacksmiths	623	470
*Shoemakers	426	272
*Shipbuilding	215	162
*Coopers	207	107
*Carriage Builders	161	156
Millers	160	164
*Tin & Coppersmiths	132	111
Painters & Glazers	117	137
*Cabinet & Furniture Makers	102	69
*Saddle & Harness Makers	97	80
*Carders *Weavers	91	85
Butchers	45	55
*Decline		

Total Manufacturing & Industrial (excluding Farming & Fishing)   1881 — 6,388
1891 — 5,321

Net Decline   1,067

Financing for the industries which developed on the Island and in the other Maritime colonies immediately before and after confederation came from independent Maritime banks including the Bank of Prince Edward Island and the Merchant's Bank of Prince Edward Island. As the competition from centralised industry forced the Maritime industries to go under, the banks went under with them. The central Canadian banks expanded into the region but rather than invest in local industries they

Steam Engine: *One of the early railway locomotives used on the Island. It was fuelled by coal which was carried in the coal car immediately behind the engine.* (PAPEI).

Blacksmith: *An Island blacksmith; there was at least one in every town.* (PAPEI).

drained savings from the Maritimes for investment in central
Canada and building grain production and trade in the newly
opened farmlands of the Prairies. The Bank of Prince Edward
Island collapsed in 1881 and the Merchant's Bank followed in
1906. Their demise cut off the financial resources needed for
development. This relegated the Island to being a resource base
for the economic development of central Canada and the West.

Forced Depopulation

The collapse of the shipbuilding industry, the local financial institutions and the decline of local manufacturing put over 1000
Islanders out of work. This was partially compensated for by the
expansion of fishing and farming, but hundreds left the Island to
find jobs in the New England States and Central Canada. Each
winter a few hundred went to work in the lumber camps of New
Brunswick and Maine.

Attached to the comprador bourgeoisie of central Canada were
the merchant middlemen. They had replaced the small Island
capitalists, who had fought to keep the Island out of confederation, in the seat of political power in Charlottetown. It was with a
feeling of defeat that Lawrence Doyle wrote this song in 1889.

> There is a band within this land
> Who live in pomp and pride;
> To swell their store they rob the poor;
> On pleasure's wings they ride.
> With dishes fine their tables shine
> They live in princely style.
> They are the knaves who made us slaves
> And sold Prince Edward Isle.
>
> Through want and care and scanty fare,
> The poor man drags along:
> He hears a whistle loud and shrill,
> The Iron Horse speeds on.
> He throws his pack upon his back,
> There's nothing left to do
> He boards the train for Bangor, Maine
> Prince Edward Island Adieu. [3]

The Conservatives controlled Island politics until the 1890's.

J.C. Pope's nephew became the private secretary of John A. Macdonald, a symbol of the bond which existed between the provincial and federal policy makers.

The Island's population reached a peak of 109,078 in 1891, but the loss of jobs resulted in a rapid decline in population which continued well into the twentieth century. By 1931 only 88,038 people lived on the Island and the 1891 level was not reached again until the mid-1960's.

Population P.E.I.			
1881	1891	1901	1911
108,891	109,078	103,259	93,728

Chapter Notes

1. *Journal of the House of Aseembly*, for years 1846 to 1873 inclusive. *Sessional Papers, Dominion of Canada* for year 1874 and onward.
2. *Dominion Bureau of Statistics Reports*, for years 1881 and 1891. PAC.
3. Lawrence Doyle, "P.E.I. Adieu" in Edward Ives, *Lawrence Doyle—The Farmer Poet of Prince Edward Island*, Orno, University of Maine, 1971.

17

The politics of education and religion

The School System

Although the controversy over religious teaching in the public school system that had been such a prominent political issue in the 1858 and 1863 elections had died down by 1870, the tensions between the politically and economically dominant Protestants and the politically and economically deprived Roman Catholics never abated.

The Free Education Act of 1852 provided for a minimal elementary education and teaching offered a professional career to those who could not become doctors or lawyers or pursue another profession. The quality of education was not high and teachers were extremely poorly paid. Many were local residents whose own education was little better than that of their students.

In 1874, school inspector William MacPhail, himself receiving only two hundred dollars a year, wrote this description of a visit to a Charlottetown school

> Many of the pupils were never long at one school, but keep running from school to school ... At the Temperance Hall [location of one of the schools] I found pupils who had been attending at six different schools during the past six months. At the Hillsborough School, there were found pupils from four different schools in [sic] the same time. At Scott's Hall, on the day of my visit, there were 94 pupils in attendance, of whom 48 had attended nine different schools during the past six months ...[1]

Many of the schools were little more than meeting places where young people came to socialise and torment their teachers. There was no discipline and little learning occurred. This situation did not change until a new education act was introduced in 1877. The new act not only introduced a uniform system of education, but increased the salaries of teachers, thus attracting better qualified people to the profession. In the first year and a half after the new act was passed, school attendance increased by five thousand. In the years following, a high percentage of Island young people received at least a minimum education.

The Separate School Question

In 1875 the issue of religious education in the public schools erupted yet again.

The Catholic clergy, anxious to maintain their traditional control over their parishioners, wanted to establish a separate school system financed by public funds. Most Protestants opposed this scheme.

Although the 1852 Free Education Act explicitly precluded religious teaching in public schools, it was carried on in many districts, especially in rural areas. In 1874, 56 of the 143 schools in Queen's County, 36 Catholic and 18 Protestant, were using either the shorter (Protestant) or Butler's (Catholic) catechism for religious instruction.

In Charlottetown, teachers in the denominational schools run by Methodist, Anglican and Catholic churches were receiving pay from the public treasury. Those who opposed the separate school system charged that the School Board was making a mockery out of the School Act and demanded that the practices stop. Those who favored the separate school system argued for making official what was already happening in practice.

The 1876 election was fought exclusively on the question of separate schools. Members of both the Liberal and Conservative parties crossed party lines to line up on one side or the other.

The Secular School party was led by Louis Davies, a Liberal and the Separate School party by W.W. Sullivan, a Conservative. Davis became the new premier and introduced the new School

Act in 1877.

However, the question was not settled by government legislation but through a series of compromises worked out by the people. A number of schools, although officially public, were in fact denominational. This occurred in urban centres where all Catholics went to one school and all Protestants to another.

In smaller rural districts where it was not possible to have two schools, it was agreed to alternate teachers along religious lines, Catholic following Protestant and vice versa.

This system continued until very recent times. As recently as 1965, Protestant junior high school students in Charlottetown went to Queen Charlotte school on one side of the city and Catholic students to Birchwood on the other. In the past ten years consolidation has forced the closure of most of the smaller schools and students from both denominations have been integrated.

The Rural District Schools

The great majority of rural schools were one-room buildings. In these one-room schools teachers laboured to teach up to fifty children ranging in age from six to sixteen. It was common practice for older boys to attend schools from December till March during the season when their labour was not needed on the farm.

One of the weaknesses in this system was the method by which teachers were paid. In addition to the salary from the government, each district offered a further salary called a supplement. Of course the wealthier districts offered higher supplements and got the best teachers. This system saved the government money but it fostered and perpetuated inequality in education.

In the rural areas the school districts were the centres of community life. The community people had responsibility for the upkeep of the school and each year elected a Board of School Trustees for this purpose. Trustees, like teachers, were elected according to religion with Catholics and Protestants alternating.

Each district had its own branch of the Women's Institute* which looked after the upkeep of the school and other community projects. Each district also had its own sports teams which engaged in competition, sometimes not so friendly, with neigh-

*Federated Women's Institutes of Canada.

bouring districts.

Chapter Notes

1. In H. B. Matthews, "Education in Prince Edward Island", M.A. thesis, Mount Allison University, 1938.

18

People's organisations—cooperatives and trade unions

Co-operation—A Way of Life

Perhaps the Island people's attitude toward co-operatives is best expressed in the words of a farmer who, when asked by a magazine writer if co-operative Marketing Associations operated in his community said, "No, I don't think so." After describing egg co-ops, shipping co-ops and co-operative creameries he said to his puzzled questioner, "I guess maybe you'd call what we're doing here cooperative marketing, but I thought you meant something done on a great magnificent scale. All we're doing here is working together in a simple sort of way, as a group of neighbours should, in order to get our stuff to market." [1]

That modest description of the Co-ops formed by the farmers and fishermen illustrates admirably their co-operative spirit. It was their way to defeat their exploitation by the merchants who drained off their profits.

Co-operation was not new to the farmers and fishermen of the mid nineteenth century. The earliest residents, the Micmac and the Acadiens, used co-operative methods in their day to day lives. Early settlers had always co-operated to build roads and barns, to maintain the schools and to organise community entertainment. The first Islanders to organise co-operatives for commercial purposes were the Acadiens who formed the Farmer's Bank of Rustico in 1863, and the Acadien Grain Banks in 1869.

Farmer's Bank: *Situated in South Rustico, the bank served the surrounding community for thirty years between 1864 and 1894. The building is built of Island sandstone. (Private Collection).*

The Farmer's Bank

In 1864, very few of the Acadien farmers of Rustico owned their own land. They did not have the money to make down payments on land even to the landlords who were prepared to sell. It was not uncommon for farmers to be jailed for non-payment of rent.

The farmers were unable to borrow money from the commercial banks, The Merchant's Bank, The Bank of Prince Edward Island and the Union Bank, which were controlled by the merchants. When money was available from money lenders, they could not afford the ten to twelve percent demanded in interest.

In 1863, they decided to establish their own bank. In that year, they petitioned the Island government for a charter to incorporate. The Act of Incorporation received royal assent in 1864 and that same year the bank's doors were opened to business. (The bank building, which still stands, was built by the farmers from blocks of Island sandstone.) The farmer-members of the bank issued and themselves bought shares valued at one pound sterling each. The members appointed from among themselves a board of directors, a supervisory committee, and a credit committee. The first president was Jerome Doiron and the first cashier, Maren Blanchard.

In its thirty years of existence, the bank's assets never exceeded $4,000. It made loans to farmers, usually never more than forty dollars, at low interest rates, for down payments on land or farm improvements.

In its first year of operation twelve percent interest was paid on deposits. This later had to be lowered, first to ten and later to eight percent, because only six percent was charged for loans.

The bank proved so beneficial to people in Rustico that it wasn't long before people from as far away as Egmont Bay, Miscouche and Tignish became members and each week sent a representative to Rustico to do business.

Until the Farmer's Bank started printing bank notes, the little currency there was on the Island was in the hands of the merchants. Now for the first time farmers had money in their hands with which to buy consumer goods. This gave them a degree of independence and control over their own businesses which they never had before. The notes from the bank circulated as far away as Montreal.

When the bank's original charter ran out in 1883, the directors had to go to the federal parliament to have it renewed. They were not well received because the federal government was pursuing a policy of closing down small banks. It wanted to concentrate capital in a few national chartered banks so that the economy would be centralised in the hands of the new imperialist compradors, in Montreal and Toronto.

The people in Rustico, led by the parish priest, Father Belcourt, insisted that the charter be renewed. Belcourt argued:

> ... the farmer is the man who really creates wealth, he is the nourishing father of the body politic; from him the baker gets his flour, the weaver his yarn, the shoemaker his leather, and the butcher his beef, and of all the members of society the farmer is the one who bears the heaviest burden; thus he needs an income which will sustain him. Take this bank from the farmer and you will be throwing him to the rapacious clutches of the usurer, the social bloodsucker who

holds in misery that interesting class of people, the farmer. There is only one type of bank which can lend small sums as well as large amounts at moderate rates of interest, and which can come to the farmer's aid and help to secure good land. [2]

The people's insistence that the bank must continue convinced the federal government to renew the charter in spite of a regulation requiring a bank to have $555,000 assets before obtaining a charter. The Farmer's Bank had only $3,900.

Still the bank was doomed. Requests for charters for similar banks in Summerside and Souris were denied. The commercial banks on the Island refused to cash the notes issued by the Farmer's Bank. As a result it faded away in the early 1890's but not before it had paved the way for the credit union movement which came thirty-five years later and inspired Alphonse Desjardins to organise the first Caisse Populaire at Levis, Québec, in 1900.

In the end the small commercial banks, the Merchant's Bank, the Union Bank and the Bank of Prince Edward Island were forced into bankruptcy or gobbled up in turn by the large chartered banks as centralisation of the economy continued.

The Grain Banks

In 1868, an "Act for the Incorporation of Societies for the sale and distribution of Seed Grains, on credit" was passed in the Island legislature.

The first society to be incorporated under the act was the Abram's Seed Club in Abram's Village, January 8, 1869. By 1879 at least 24 societies had been formed. With one exception—that of Lot 11, St. Bridgit Grain Society—all were formed in Acadien communities. There was at least one grain bank in every Acadien parish.

Like the Farmer's Bank these societies were formed to give credit to farmers who could not get or could not afford credit from other sources.

A typical society might include from thirty to fifty farmers living in a neighbourhood. Those with a surplus of seed grain would "invest" it in "shares" in the society. Ten bushels would

usually constitute one share. The grain—usually oats, though a
little barley and occasionally some wheat were used—would be
stored through a winter in a building belonging to the society and
in the spring would be lent to farmers who needed seed. For every
bushel borrowed, a farmer, after threshing in the fall, would
return a bushel and a peck. While the "shareholders" received a
dividend, in grain, for their investment, the dividends were often
small because the societies seldom forced payment from defaulting farmers who had a bad year. In a normal year some hundreds
of bushels remained unpaid in each society. Expenses of the society were met from the sale of grain from the reserve before "dividends" were paid.[3]

Most of the Grain Banks had gone out of business by the 1920's
when the movement away from trade and barter to cash trans-
actions made them obsolete. However, the last society, the
Egmont Bay Road Seed Club continued in business until 1946. It
had been in existence for seventy-seven years.

Other Co-operatives

The development of Co-ops was not limited to the Acadien communities. The first dairy cooperative was established by Dr. James
W. Robertson in New Perth in the spring of 1892. In its first year
of operation it turned out 66,080 pounds of cheese. The idea
spread. In 1893 co-operatives were formed at Crapaud, Dunk
River, Gowan Brae, Kensington, Morell, Mount Stewart, Murray
Harbour North, Red House-Lot 56, St. Peter's Bay and Vernon
Bridge. Eventually the number of factories reached 40.[4] Not one
of these co-operative dairies remains today although those at
Morell and Kinkora continued until the early 1970's. They were
all bought out by larger commercial dairies or were acquired
by local businessmen.

The co-operative dairies had been operating for twenty years
when farmers started forming egg circles to market eggs. The first
egg circle was formed at Brooklyn in 1913 and the first shipment
of eggs to be marketed under the system was made from the New
London egg circle in May of 1913. By 1931 there were 61 egg
circles with 3,800 members (one for every 23 Islanders in that

year). In 1940 the egg circles which had been chartered under the Prince Edward Island Co-operative Egg and Poultry Association collapsed, victims of mismanagement by the Association's own directors and a crisis of confidence among members.

Yet another co-operative venture was the Prince Edward Island Potato Growers' Association founded in 1920. Under the direction of J. Wilfred Boulter, the Association was formed to improve the industry, standardize grades, promote better marketing and eradicate disease. By 1930 the Association was marketing seed potatoes to the eastern and Gulf ports of the United States, to Cuba and other countries. The volume of trade reached over 1.4 million bushels of potatoes valued at $2.7 million.

The Association broke down when private dealers purposely took losses to price it out of the market. It was finally finished off by the Liberal government of Alex Matheson and replaced with the non-producer controlled Potato Marketing Board in 1956.

The farmers also formed shipping clubs for the marketing of pigs, lambs, wool and other products.

The Fishermen Organise

Fishermen got together to form co-operatives in the early 1900's. Fishing was a risky business at best because, as Rustico fisherman Bertram Blaquiere recalls: "There are few industries in which a person can work six months and earn a living. Fishing is no exception. Added to this," he says, "is the strange fact that fishing is one of the few industries where the entire risk of loss is borne by the worker. The middleman, or dealer, will handle fish only when there is a profit; and this profit is taken first whether the price is high or low." Good seasons' earnings were taken to pay the debts (to the middleman) of the bad years. The fishermen found themselves in an inflexible relationship with the merchants. "Naturally," says Blaquiere, "the merchant who bought the fish made a profit on them. Not only did he make a profit on the sale of fish, but also on the sale of gear to the fishermen. The fishermen could not win in this game, where they sold their fish at a low price and then bought their supplies at a high price. No industry organized in such a way could hope to be profitable. The fishermen, as a matter of fact, found it almost impossible to provide their families with the bare necessities of life." [5]

In 1909, the Rustico fishermen rented a factory and for a time did their own packing. This was the first step toward co-operative marketing but they did not gain complete control of packing and marketing until the formation of Fishermen's Unions in 1923. The first union was established in Tignish, to be incorporated as Station No. 1, under "An Act to Provide for the Organization of Fishermen's Unions" passed in the legislature in 1925. The president of this first union was Chester McCarthy, a lawyer with fishing experience. McCarthy became the first president of the United Maritime Fishermen but, in 1933, led the Island Fishermen's Union out of the UMF because the mainlanders neglected the special interests of Island fishermen.

By 1941 there were 28 separate unions on the Island. They effectively cut out the middlemen and thus the fishermen's dependency on the merchants. By collective marketing and buying of supplies, they were able to turn the profits to their own advantage. As a result of these unions other co-operatives were formed to assist the fishing villages in other purchases. Today Tignish has five co-operative associations providing services in marketing and retail trade.

The Trade Union Movement Begins

While the fishermen and farmers were taking steps to improve their position by taking control of their local economy, workers on the Island began to organise trade unions to get better wages and working conditions for themselves.

Workers, unlike fishermen and farmers, owned no property. All they had to sell was their labour. While farmers and fishermen owned the products they produced until they were sold, the products produced by the workers were the property of their employers. Farmers and fishermen organised to negotiate the prices they were to get for their products. Workers organised to negotiate the conditions under which they worked and the price they were to be paid for their labour.

The first union was a Canadian union, the Railway Employees'

Federal Labour Union, Local 10, chartered in Charlottetown in 1899.

In 1901, Local 10 was represented at the convention of the Trades and Labour Congress of Canada by George W. Worthy. At that time Local 10 was the only Canadian union on P.E.I.; the other three locals being affiliated to the American Federation of Labour.

Worthy asked the congress to send an organiser to P.E.I. assuring TLC leaders that other unions could be formed if this were done. The Canadian congress did not send an organiser but the American Federation of Labour sent John Flett of Hamilton who organised nine new AFL affiliated unions. The AFL unions then formed the Charlottetown Trades and Labour Council which refused to admit unions chartered by the TLC. This greatly angered the TLC unions. Led by Worthy, these unions were strongly of the opinion that Trades and Labour Councils in Canada should be chartered by the Canadian Union centre.

Union Locals in P.E.I.[6]			
Year	*Number*	*Year*	*Number*
1900	1	1905	10
1901	4	1906	6
1902	16	1907	6
1903	11	1908	7
1904	11	1909	8

While the TLC unions in Charlottetown battled with the AFL Trades and Labour Council, the issue came up for debate at the 1902 TLC Convention in Berlin (Kitchener), Ontario.

At this convention the AFL affiliate unions demanded that the TLC throw out all unions which were "dual" to the AFL unions. The Congress passed an amendment to the TLC constitution specifying that "no National Union be recognised where an International Union exists."[7] This amendment caused a split when the National Unions deemed by the AFL to be dual unions were ousted. In 1903 the National Trades and Labour Council was formed as a separate labour council to fight for Canadian Unions. The Berlin conference marked the beginning of the struggle for independent Canadian Unions which have been a part of Canadian labour history ever since.

Unions on P.E.I. — 1902[8]	
AFL Unions	*TLC Unions*
Carpenters & Joiners	Railway Employees No. 10
Painters & Decorators	3 Railway Trackmen
Printers	3 Federal Labour Unions
Tobacco Workers	
Railway Telegraphers	9 American Federation of Labour
Railway Trackmen	7 Trades and Labour Congress
Truckmen	
2 Federal Labour Unions	

In Charlottetown, unions chartered by the TLC were not classified as dual unions and in 1904 were admitted to the Charlottetown Trades and Labour Council. However the Council and all but two of the sixteen unions in existence in 1902 were short lived. Lack of support from the American parent bodies for these unions was a major factor in their demise.

The two surviving unions were the Labourer's Protective Union (LPU) and the Railway Employees Union. The LPU, a longshoreman's union, broke away from the AFL in 1904 and became independent because, as one LPU member said, "the international would do nothing for us."[9] As an independent union it became strong. Relying solely on its members, it succeeded in getting all the companies on the Charlottetown waterfront to meet its demands concerning conditions. From time to time attempts were made to bring in dock workers below union wage rates but each time the LPU stood its ground and won. This union was the most militant and class conscious of all the unions which existed in 1902.

The LPU also worked to organise other workers. In 1907, the workers who hauled coal from the Charlottetown wharves were organised with the assistance of the LPU into a truckmen's union and in 1912 the LPU led attempts to organise the firemen, an effort that never succeeded.

One of the most colourful and exciting events in Charlottetown in the early years of this century was the annual Labour Day parade initiated and organised by the LPU. People from many parts of the Island took part. In 1907, a band from Souris, fifty miles away, came to the celebration. Following the 1907 parade a member of the LPU said "the spirit of Unionism is still alive and vigorous in the LPU, where other organisations have failed it was still in the front and growing stronger."[10] He urged the members to keep on and by example encourage other workers to organise.

The LPU also organised a sick benefit plan some forty years before workman's compensation was introduced on the Island. The LPU is an excellent example of "the spirit of brotherhood" which had died in the American controlled unions. As a militant local union dedicated to its members the LPU succeeded unlike the rich international unions that failed. History gives many examples of that lesson.

Co-operation is a basic human response to the challenges of scarcity, hardship, danger and the more routine concerns like earning a living, and entertaining oneself. For Islanders it was a way of achieving producer-controlled and worker-controlled organisations that would give the farmers, fishermen and workers a larger share of the profits of their labours. The organisations did not break the hold that the comprador merchants had over the province, but they did assist the people in their struggle for their own well-being. We will see later how many of their organisations were destroyed and how the people again organise themselves to fight against oppression.

Population 1911   93,728

Chapter Notes

1. Robin Hood, "The Denmark of Canada" in *Cooperative Marketing Journal*, March-April, 1931. P.E.I. Collection, University of P.E.I.
2. Theophilus Blanchard, from a speech delivered at the 25th Anniversary of the St. Augustine's Credit Union, South Rustico, 1963.
3. John T. Croteau, "The Acadian Grain Banks of Prince Edward Island" in *Agricultural History*, July, 1955. P.E.I. Collection, University of P.E.I.

4. A. Gary Webster, "The Denmark of Canada? The Place of Co-operation, Co-operatives and Credit Unions in Island Socio-economic History", P.E.I. Collection, University of P.E.I.
5. Bertram A. Blanchard, *What Fishermen Can Do: The Story of North Rustico*. Charlottetown, The Adult Education League of P.E.I., 1940. Public Archives, P.E.I.
6. Eugene Forsey, "Some Notes on the Early History of Unions in P.E.I.", *Canadian Historical Review*, Vol. XLVI, No. 4, December 1965.
7. Charles Lipton, *The Trade Union Movement of Canada, 1827-1959,* Toronto, NC Press, 1973, p. 132.
8. *Ibid.*, Forsey.
9. Labourer's Protective Union "Minute Book", LPU office, Charlottetown.
10. Ibid.

19

A farmer's diary

A Year on the Farm

The following diary was kept by the author's father for the year 1918. It offers an insight into the life of a P.E.I. farmer before the days of modern communication and electricity. Even as recently as 50 years ago, following the upheavals of a world war and the social revolution in Russia, the farmers of P.E.I. lived in communities barely touched by the outside world.

January 1918

1. Fine and cold, six below; killed the ox. (*1*)
2. Fine, school started.
3. Very cold, Peter Sinclair's house burnt. Storming in evening.
4. Soft, raining all day. (*2*)
5. Fine and mild.
6. Fine and mild.
7. Fine and mild.
8. Raining, Papa went to Bradalbane.
9. Fine.
10. Fine, coasting on Mort's hill. (*3*)
11. Fine.
12. Fine, Papa and me to Summerside.
13. Fine, with snow shower.
14. Fine.
15. Storming in evening.
16. Drifting bad. (*4*)

17. Fine.
18. Fine, Started mud. (*5*)
19. Fine, set traps in R.B. ('s) brook. (*6*)
20. Fine in forenoon, squally in afternoon.
21. Fine.
22. Fine.
23. Snowing some.
24. Cold & drifting.
25. Fine.
26. Mild & snowing.
27. Fine & very cold.
28. Fine and very cold, 9 below zero, threshing. (*7*)
29. Fine.
30. Fine and cold.
31. Fine.

(*1*) All of the meat eaten on the farm came from animals slaughtered by the farmers. Any excess part of the meat would be sold or more likely bartered with a neighbour.

(*2*) In P.E.I. it was normal for the snow to come and go two or three times during the winter. Farmers referred to this as a *thaw* or *soft spell*.

(*3*) A favorite recreation was sliding down a hill in a sleigh or toboggan called *coasting*.

(*4*) The weather was always of concern. When it snowed rural people were unable to travel. After a storm each farmer had to break his share of the road.

(*5*) Each winter the farmers went to the river with sleighs to buy mud dragged from the river bottom which they spread on their land for fertilizer. Before farmers started using mud in the 1840's the lime-poor soil produced only marginal crops. The lime-rich mud was a very important ingredient which turned otherwise marginal land into what is some of the best land in North America.

(*6*) It was customary for rural people to set traps each winter to capture fur bearing animals. The furs were then sold.

(*7*) In the fall grain or wheat was stored in the barn in sheaves to be threshed as needed during the winter months.

Mudding: *The mud was scraped from the river bed and loaded on sleighs or wagons to be hauled and spread on the new land. The lime rich mud turned the otherwise marginal land into some of the best land in North America. Farmers paid for the mud by the load. (PAPEI).*

February 1918

1. Fine and cold.
2. Fine and cold, Jim Glover buried. (*1*)
3. Fine and cold.
4. Snow in morning, fine in afternoon.
5. Cold and drifting.
6. Very cold, 12 below zero.
7. Cold.
8. Clear and cold.
9. Fine.
10. Fine.
11. Fine.
12. Little stormy.
13. Fine.
14. Fine and mild.
15. Mild and thawing.
16. Fine.
17. Fine.
18. Fine and drifting.
19. Drifting.
20. Cold and blowing.

Hauling wood: *Each year trees were cut into logs which were later cut into 18-inch blocks to be split into firewood in preparation for use as fuel.* (*PAPEI*).

21. Cold.
22. Very cold, coldest this winter.
23. Storming a little.
24. Fine.
25. Fine, started hauling mud.
26. Raining in afternoon.
27. Fine and cold.
28. Fine, hauling grain.

(*1*) While deaths were mourned by everyone in the community they are just recorded in the diary with no comment.

March 1918

1. Fine.
2. Fine.
3. Blowing hard, drifting.
4. Fine and cold.
5. Fine, hauling mud.
6. Storming.
7. Cold wind.

8. Cold, 14 below.
9. Lovely & warm.
10. Stormy, bad storm at night.
11. Drifting bad.
12. Fine.
13. Drifting.
14. Fine.
15. Storming.
16. Drifting bad.
17. Fine.
18. Fine & drifting.
19. Fine.
20. Fine.
21. Elegant, finished mud.
22. South wind, fine. (*1*)
23. Drifting.
24. High wind, went to Church.
25. Fine.
26. Fine, saw bluebird. (*1*)
27. Fine, saw greybird. (*1*)
28. Fine.
29. Fine.
30. Fine.
31. Fine.

(*1*) The south wind and the appearance of birds were always signs of approaching spring and were duly noted by the farmers who were preparing for spring planting.

April 1918

1. Lovely day, first robin.
2. Fine.
3. Fine.
4. Fine.
5. Stormy.
6. Fine, threshing.
7. Fine.
8. Fine.
9. Fine.
10. Very cold and windy, took out pigs. (*1*)
11. Fine.
12. Fine.
13. Raining a little.

14. Fine.
15. Fine.
16. Fine.
17. Fine.
18. Fine.
19. Fine.
20. Fine.
21. Raining some.
22. Raining, first wagon, first mail. (2)
23. Fine.
24. Fine.
25. Fine.
26. Fine, cleaning seed. (3)
27. Fine, cutting shingle wood. (4)
28. Fine, Aunt Mary died.
29. Fine, cutting wood. (5)
30. Rained, funeral.

(1) In winter, pigs that were ready to send to market were taken to Kensington, the nearest town, where they were sold to a produce dealer.

(2) The appearance of a wagon and the mail were a welcomed sight—it meant that the snow was almost all gone and planting time was near.

(3) Each spring the seed grain had to be cleaned in preparation for sowing.

(4) Shingles were made from wood cut in the woodlot which was part of every farm.

(5) Each year the wood used for fuel in the farm house had to be cut from the woodlot, sawed into approximately 18 inch lengths and split with an axe so it would go into the stove.

May 1918

1. Raining.
2. Fine, Ewen Walker's sale. (1)
3. Fine, digging stones. (2)
4. Fine, picking P. [potatoes] in cellar. (3)
5. Fine.
6. Showery.
7. Fine, putting in posts. (4)
8. Fine, hauling potatoes. (5)

Haymaking: *Above, the hay was cut and then piled into piles, called coils, to dry. It was common practice for all members of the family to work in the fields to get the hay stored before it got wet or spoiled. Below, loading the hay by hand in preparation for hauling it to the hay barn for storage.* (PAPEI).

9. Fine, manure turnips. (6)
10. Fine.
11. Showery.
12. Fine.
13. Commenced to harrow. (7)
14. Fine.
15. Fine.
16. Fine, sowing wheat and barley.
17. Sowing oats.
18. Fine.
19. Fine, went for Fanny. (8)
20. Fine.
21. Sowing oats on Cobb place. (9)
22. Fine.
23. Rain in afternoon and evening.
24. Sewing.
25. Finished sewing.
26. Fine.
27. Finished harrowing.
28. Wet.
29. Fine, fencing on Harrington place.
30. Fine.
31. Fine.

(1) When a farmer went out of business, all his property including the land, was sold by auction. These sales were as much a social event as a business event.

(2) Although the land was cleared, each year new stones appeared and had to be removed.

(3) Grading the potatoes in preparation for market.

(4) Each year the fences damaged during the winter had to be repaired.

(5) Taking the potatoes to a potato dealer to sell.

(6) Each spring the manure was spread on the land where the root crops, turnips, mangels and potatoes, were to be planted.

(7) Preparing the land for planting.

(8) Probably drove to the rail station to pick up Fanny, a relative coming for a visit.

(9) Parts of the farm had been purchased from another man and afterward were identified by his name.

June 1918

1. Fine, rain at night.
2. Lovely day.
3. Fine, took out cow.
4. Fine.
5. Fine, planting potatoes.
6. Fine, potatoes.
7. Planting, raining in evening.
8. Fine, finished potatoes, put in grain.
9. Fine.
10. Fine.
11. Fine.
12. Sewed turnips, rained hard in afternoon.
13. Rain showers and thunder.
14. Fine.
15. Fine.
16. Fine.
17. Showery.
18. Fine, hauling logs for shingles.
19. Started hauling mud.
20. Fine.
21. Fine, hauling logs for registered boards. (*1*)
22. Skinned heffer that died. (*2*)
23. Fine, cold in afternoon.
24. Fine, Lindsay whiting pig house. (*3*)
25. Fine, cold in afternoon.
26. Fine and cool.
27. Fine.
28. Stanley went west. (*4*)
29. Fine.
30. Rain in morning, W.S. Hogg buried.

(*1*) Registered boards were boards sawed with interlocking grooves so they would match together.

(*2*) The hides from cattle went to the tannery to make leather.

(*3*) Whitewashing, most of the buildings, other than the house, were whitewashed annually.

(*4*) My father's brother. Many of the young men went to western Canada during the summer on the harvest excursion to work in the wheat fields.

July 1918

1. Nice, a few showers.
2. Fine.
3. Very warm, lovely rain in evening. Commenced shingling Ade's barn.
4. Raining, was to be an ice-cream social at R. Bowness' but too wet. (*1*)
5. Fine, cream social came off.
6. W.H. and Lindsay to Summerside, shingling at Ade's.
7. Fine, Sunday.
8. Very heavy rain, first day to sell milk.
9. Fine.
10. Fine, finished mud.
11. Heavy thunder storm, hail in south, afternoon very warm.
12. Very warm.
13. Very warm, finished turnips.
14. Heavy rain.
15. Fine.
16. Fine.
17. Fine.
18. Lovely, out fishing.
19. Fine.

20. Fine, shower in evening.
21. Fine.
22. Fine.
23. Fine while washing 'till evening, heavy thunder and rain. (*2*)
24. Fine, Kensington for hay loader.
25. Commenced cutting hay.
26. Fine.
27. Took in hay, heavy thunder at night.
28. Fine.
29. Fine.
30. Fine.
31. Fine, day of troubles.

(*1*) One of the more enjoyable social occasions was the ice-cream social. People from the whole community got together to enjoy home-made ice cream. The proceeds went to the group putting it on, usually the Women's Auxiliary or the Women's Institute. *The Auxiliary* was a group connected with the Church which kept the Church building cleaned and decorated. *The Institute* fulfilled much the same role for the school.

(2) Once a week, on Monday if fine, the farm women did the family washing. They always looked for a fine day so that the clothes would dry.

August 1918

1. Fine, put in 11 loads of hay, cool day.
2. Fine, working at hay.
3. Rained in morning, spraying potatoes.
4. Sunday, lovely day.
5. Fine in forenoon, rained in afternoon, cutting hay at Ade's.
6. Fine, cutting hay in afternoon.
7. Fine, putting in hay.
8. Fine, putting in hay, finished at Ade's.
9. Fine, finished cutting hay.
10. Fine, William Denis funeral.
11. Fine.
12. Rained in forenoon, digging stones, spraying potatoes.
13. Fine.
14. Fine, finished hay, rain and thunder in evening.
15. Fine.
16. Fine.
17. Fine.
18. Fine.
19. Fine, putting out manure.
20. Fine.
21. Fine.
22. Fine, finished Paris green. (1)
23. Fine, started stumping. (2)
24. Fine, stumping.
25. Fine.
26. Fine, stumping.
27. Showery, stumping.
28. Fine.
29. Fine.
30. Fine, ice cream at Geo. Glover's.
31. Fine, at Harry Bowness' for ice cream.

(1) Paris green was the material used for spraying potatoes.

(2) There was still land to be cleared. After the trees were cut the stumps were removed from the land. It was then plowed and mudded in preparation for cropping.

September 1918

1. Lovely showers.
2. Fine, hauling stumps.
3. Fine, hauling stones, took in barley, Laura at H. Warren's.
4. Fine, cutting [grain] on hill.
5. Fine, cutting front fields.
6. Cut wheat.
7. Rained in morning.
8. Fine.
9. Rained hard in forenoon, Summerfield in afternoon, commenced to plow.
10. Fine, cutting at Ade's.
11. Fine, cutting, very cold.
12. Fine, cutting, heavy frost this morning.
13. Fine, finished cutting.
14. Fine, in Summerside.
15. Fine, Margate church reopened.
16. Fine, taking in grain.
17. Fine, took in wheat.
18. Raining. (*1*)
19. Fine.
20. Fine, finished at Ade's.
21. Very wet.
22. Fine, rained at night.
23. Fine, taking in oats.
24. Fine.
25. Fine, plowing garden. (*2*)
26. Fine, finished harvest.
27. Heavy rain, at Ade's making doors.
28. Blowing hard.
29. Fine.
30. Fine, at Ade's putting in grain.

(*1*) The grain was cut and stooked. After a day's rain they had to wait a day for the grain to dry.

(*2*) Although the garden is only mentioned in relation to plowing, it was a very important part of farm life. Each spring the farm women planted the garden and in the fall gathered the vegetables and other products to preserve them for use during the winter.

<u>Harvest:</u> *The grain was cut and bound into sheaves which were then piled into a stukes to dry and later hauled to be threshed or stored in the barn. Below, threshing the grain. The straw (grain stalks) was piled to be later stored and used in the barns to 'bed' the farm animals. (PAPEI).*

October 1918

1. Started to plow at Ade's.
2. Fine, plowing.
3. Raining, plowing in afternoon.
4. Fine, threshing at father's.
5. Wet, Colledge Brown's sale.
6. Rained all day.
7. Rained in forenoon, Lindsay went to Wesley's in evening.
8. Fine.
9. Fine.
10. Fine, threshing at Geo Sharpe's.
11. Fine, to mill with wheat. (*1*)
12. Fine, plowing.
13. Fine.
14. Commenced potatoes.
15. Fine, at potatoes.
16. Fine, at potatoes.
17. Fine, finished potatoes.
18. Fine, plowing and stumping at Ade's.
19. Fine, plowing and stumping.
20. Fine, went for Dr. [Doctor] for grandpa.
21. Rained in afternoon, Lindsay went to Eddison's.
22. Plowing, rained in afternoon.
23. Drisley.
24. Fine, plowing.
25. Fine.
26. Rained in afternoon, Lindsay came from Edith's.
27. Fine.
28. Fine, finished plowing at Ade's.
29. Fine, started to plow back field.
30. Rained in afternoon.
31. Rained all day.

(*1*) The wheat was taken to the mill to be ground into flour.

November 1918

1. Fine.
2. Taking in turnips.
3. Fine, some showers.
4. Showery, plowed potato land.
5. Fine, plowing.
6. Fine, plowing.
7. Fine, finished plowing, Peace declared—word false report.

Mill: *One of many mills which were run by water power. Mills were built to grind grain as well as saw logs into lumber. Note the dam and mill pond where the water was backed up to supply enough pressure to run the mill. Note also the sumps left after the land was cleared. They were later removed.* (Private Collection).

8. Showery, digging stones at Ade's.
9. Fine, killed Maria's pig.
10. Fine, showers in afternoon.
11. Peace declared, Fine, plowing at Eddison's.
12. Bought Sheen farm. (*1*)
13. Digging stones, threshing, out with oats.
14. Very stormy, took in young cattle. (*2*)
15. Fine.
16. To Summerside settling for farm, took out oats.
17. Fine.
18. Fine, banking house, Stanley at Mort's. (*3*)
19. Wet, threshing.
20. Fine, hauling logs to mill. (*4*)
21. Fine, hauling logs.
22. Getting wood out of father's woods.
23. Snow showery, hauling out manure.
24. Very fine.
25. Very fine, cutting wood on the Sullivan [place].
26. Very cold and blowing hard, in woods.
27. Cold, to the mill for plank.
28. Fine, hauling out wood.

Potatoes: *Digging the Island's cash crop. Each year people were employed to pick the potatoes which were then stored in the cellar (basement) of the farm house later to be graded in preparation for market. (PAPEI).*

29. Snowing and blowing.
30. Fine, in woods.

(*1*) It was during this period that the size of farms increased. Many farmers bought adjacent farms to add to their acreage.

(*2*) When it got cold the cattle were brought in from the pasture to be housed in the barn until spring.

(*3*) Each fall the house was banked with clay to keep the cellar temperature above freezing in winter. The potatoes and vegetables were stored in the cellar.

(*4*) The logs were hauled to the mill to be sawed into boards, planks and shingles.

December 1918

1. Fine, cold.
2. Cold and blowing, went to K [Kensington] to telegram Annie.
3. Fine, in woods.
4. Snowing in afternoon.
5. Fine.

6. Fine.
7. Fine.
8. Fine.
9. Fine in forenoon, snowing in evening.
10. Fine, got sick.
11. Fine, Dr. for me.
12. Fine, Dr. for me.
13. Fine, Dr. for me.
14. Fine, I got up, Stanley took sick.
15. Thawing, Dr. for Stanley and mother.
16. Fine.
17. Fine.
18. Fine.
19. Fine.
20. Fine.
21. Fine.
22. Fine.
23. Sawing wood, showery.
24. Sawing wood, snow showery.
25. Rain, silver thaw.
26. Sawing wood at Grandpas, Grandpa died at 15 to 8.
27. Snowing in morning, went to Kensington for coffin.
28. Father's funeral, stormy.
29. Stormy all day.
30. Took Mrs. Heaney home, killed pig.
31. Took pigs to Kensington, hauled first oats from Ade's.

Farm Accounts for 1918

	Receipts	Expenditures
January	$ 55.50	$ 51.42
February	33.45	54.42
March	52.43	38.56
April	246.18	151.78
May	77.15	121.55
June	172.16	173.81
July	62.64	54.77
August	408.74	212.20
September	27.81	53.17
October	71.08	78.72
November	236.91	341.59
December	357.21	29.50
Year total	1,801.26	1,362.43

20

Changing empires

Imperialist Expansion

Since the arrival of the first Europeans, Prince Edward Island had been on the periphery of the colonial hinterland of one European power or another. In the first half of the twentieth century, great changes took place in the world which profoundly affected the island. It is necessary to look at those changes in order to understand their effect upon all parts of Canada.

By the end of the nineteenth century the British Empire was world wide. But British rule was challenged by Italy and Germany, both recently unified, and by the United States, which had risen to the rank of an imperialist power.

In the pamphlet "Imperialism: The Highest Stage of Capitalism", V.I. Lenin explained that "Imperialism emerged as the development and direct continuation of the fundamental characteristics of capitalism ..."[1] Out of capitalism grows monopoly and it is necessary for the continued life of a capitalist power to expand. Expansion means colonies either by direct territorial control or by indirect economic or cultural control.

Britain took steps to ward off the new challenge and with other imperialist powers joined the rush to take over every corner of the world not already subjected to colonialism.

In 1884, at the Congress of Berlin, the European powers sat down with a map of Africa and divided up the continent among themselves. Then they occupied their new territories.

The United States won the Spanish-American War and estab
bargaining table of the Europeans. However, in 1898, on the
pretence of liberating the Spanish colonies it waged war on Spain.
The United States won the Spanish-American war and established control over much of the former Spanish Empire, including
Puerto Rico, Cuba and the Philippines.

In spite of Britain's efforts to prevent German expansion and to
maintain control of the seas, Germany expanded rapidly. Russia,
France and Austria-Hungary were also on the move.

The expanding imperialist powers maintained peace only as
long as there were unconquered territories that they could divide
among themselves. When none were left they had to wage war on
each other to redivide the colonies. In the early part of the
twentieth century they were on a collision course. Russia and
France allied with Britain against Germany and her ally
Hungary. In 1914 Germany invaded Belgium. Britain and France
declared war on Germany.

As part of the British Empire, Canada automatically entered
the war on the side of Britain. The Canadian parliament voted 50
million dollars to equip an army and called for volunteers. Canadian soldiers were placed under the command of British officers.

In the first few months of the war Germany overran Belgium
and Holland before they were stopped by the British and French
on the outskirts of Paris. The two imperialist armies then dug in
and for the next few years faced each other across a few hundred
yards called "no man's land". More troops died from disease in
the filth and mire of rat infested trenches than from bullets.

In 1917 the United States entered the war. The infusion of fresh
allied troops coupled with revolution at home forced the weakened Germans to surrender in 1918. For four years Canadian soldiers had fought and died to defend the interests of the Empire
only to return home to massive unemployment and living costs
which had doubled.

In 1917 the working class in Russia overthrew the Czar and
established the world's first socialist state. Spurred on by the Russian example, workers in Canada organised for more jobs and

improved working conditions. In 1919, 148,915 were involved in 336 strikes and lockouts. The strike movement reached its peak with the Winnipeg General Strike which brought the city to a standstill from May 15 to June 26. The Winnipeg strike was crushed by the Royal Canadian Mounted Police (R.C.M.P.) and the military under direct orders from Ottawa. However this was just the beginning of a strike and organising drive which in the next two years built the historic One Big Union across Western Canada.

Mackenzie King: Friend of Rockefeller

In 1919, the Liberals, under Mackenzie King, came to power in Ottawa and ushered in a new era.

Although the British and French were nominal winners of the war, they were both seriously crippled and deeply in debt. The real winner was the United States which entered the war late and made millions on sales and loans to fighting countries. The U.S.A. was quick to take advantage of its new strength and Canada was the first prize.

Since the time of Confederation, British interests had been successfully championed in Canada by the Conservatives, while the Liberals sought to increase U.S. influence. In 1911, the Liberals under Wilfred Laurier tried to forge a reciprocity agreement with the U.S. and were defeated at the polls.

Laurier had taken the direct approach. His campaign on the reciprocity issue tried to convince the electors that closer links with the U.S. would be good for Canada. Mackenzie King, the new champion of U.S. interests, was a different kind of politician.

In 1910, King, then Labour Minister in Laurier's cabinet, settled a strike by Grand Trunk railway workers by deceiving, splitting and misleading them with flattery, and sympathetic words while crippling their power to bargain. He achieved this by making a deal with the President of the Grand Trunk who agreed to a wage settlement in return for which King assured him that the government would allow him to fire workers who had been militant during the strike. King then turned around and

Farm Buildings: *This homestead, called "Warren Farm", is situated on the site of the French capital Port La Joie. (Private Collection).*

Ice Boats: *In winter these boats provided the only means of transportation across the Northumberland Strait separating the Island from the mainland. Passengers paid one fee if they were prepared to help push the boat over the ice and a higher fee if they just wanted to sit in the boat. (Private Collection).*

promised the strikers that the government would guarantee work for any man not rehired.

One of King's strongest supporters in the deal was James Murdock, Vice-President of the American based Brotherhood of Railway Trainmen, the striking union, who was later to become Minister of Labour in King's cabinet.

In 1914, King was hired by John D. Rockefeller Jr. as Director of Investigation into Problems of Industrial Relations. Appointed Director of Research for the Rockefeller Foundation, he launched an investigation into a union busting massacre of coal miners by one of Rockefeller's companies.

Through the efforts of King the Ludlow Massacre in Colorado was whitewashed in the eyes of the public. King told Rockefeller that "to settle the troubles in Colorado, the companies must allow their men to belong to unions."[2] Then he set up company unions whose directors were officers of the company and convinced the men that they had won their battle.

King reasoned that if the union system set up in Ludlow could settle that conflict and get production going again, why not set up a similar system in Canada. The system devised by King and in operation in every province today binds union members to a contract which cannot be broken by members during its existence under any circumstances. The labour laws also dictate a long period of conciliation and compulsory arbitration before workers can strike. Under these laws employers do not have to bargain seriously and strikes are prolonged to the detriment of the workers.

When King took office as Prime Minister in 1921, he immediately developed continentalist policies which promoted the United States' interests in Canada. American investment increased. Subsidies and tax concessions were granted to U.S. companies to develop Canadian resources rather than invest this money to develop the resources for the Canadian people.

After King retired from politics, Rockefeller showed his gratitude by presenting him with a birthday gift of $100,000 in shares "to ease any financial problems I might have in the years ahead",[3] wrote King.

From his headquarters in Ottawa King placed Canada firmly in U.S. hands. It would be some years before the full effect of this action would be felt in P.E.I.

Chapter Notes

1. V.I. Lenin, "Imperialism the Highest Stage of Capitalism", Peking, Foreign Languages Press, 1970, p. 104.
2. *The Daily Star*, Toronto, October 1919 in H.S. Ferns and B. Ostry, *The Age of Mackenzie King. London, Heinemann, 1955, p. 186.*
3. *Ibid.,* Ferns & Ostry, p. 215.

21

The years between the wars

New Masters

In 1921, United States' investment in Canada surpassed that of Britain. As U.S. influence grew, the centre of the metropolis which dominated the Canadian resource hinterland shifted from London to New York and Washington. The new absentee owners needed agents to handle their affairs in Canada. It was quite simple for the compradors who had served the British metropolis to shift their allegiance when the seat of power crossed the Atlantic.

Nationally, the agents of U.S. economic power were the politicians and senior civil servants in Ottawa and the senior managers of U.S. branch plants—many times the same people. The provinces too had their compradors. On P.E.I. they were the local merchants and their political allies busily shipping the province's resources to the metropolis and importing manufactured goods. The Island compradors were subservient to the national compradors and dealt with them rather than directly with the metropolis.

Because of the distances between manufacturer and consumer, goods on the Island were costlier than in Ontario; freight charges alone added as much as 20% to the price.

The leading merchants on the Island involved themselves in a number of local enterprises. The largest of these were the department stores of R.T. Holman Ltd. in Charlottetown and Summerside.

R. T. Holman Interests in 1923[1]		
Harry T. Holman		*J. Leroy Holman*
President	R. T. Holman Ltd.	Vice-President
President	Hall Manufacturing & Cold Storage Co.	
President	Summerside Rink Co.	
President	Park Island Silver Fox Co.	Vice-Pres.
Past Pres.	Summerside Board of Trade	Past Pres.
	Carleton Realties	President
	Maritime Board of Trade	Past President

Not all companies were locally owned. The provincial government used the people's money to assist outside monopolies to establish themselves. For example, in 1902 $150,000 and a thirty-five year tax exemption were given to a fish packing company, The Dominion Packing Co. In the words of the editor of *The P.E.I. Magazine* the government and the companies "have made up their minds to secure for themselves valuable benefits at the expense of the people of this province."[2] The party which formed the government of the day was rewarded for its generosity by donations to party funds; political patronage became traditional in Island politics.

New Industry

The Island people themselves took advantage of any new opportunity to invest in and develop local business. Such an opportunity came in the early part of the 20th century when silver fox farming was at its peak. Silver fox farming had its beginnings around the turn of the century when Charles Dalton and Robert Oulton, helped by a number of Micmac, successfully raised black and silver foxes in captivity.

A small island near Tignish, today known as Oulton's Island, was used for the first breeding operations.

The fox pelts brought high prices. In 1910 Oulton and Dalton sold 48 pelts in England at an average price of $1,000 each. Included in this sale was one pelt that fetched a record price of $2,500. Many of the pelts were sold by British merchants to the nobility of Russia.

Until 1910 fox breeding was monopolised by a group of breeders who agreed not to sell breeding animals outside their group. In addition to the Oulton-Dalton pair, the Rayners, the Tuplins and the Gordons from the Cascumpec, Alberton and Montrose areas were breeding foxes. As the price of breeding animals increased, to $25,000 a pair in 1913, the lure of instant riches broke the breeders' agreement and breeding animals were shipped to Western Canada, Ontario and the United States.

Once the break was made the industry expanded rapidly. In P.E.I., many farmers struggling to make a living in traditional farming spent their last dollar on this new venture, bought breeding stock and built fox ranches. Fur farms were concentrated in the western end of the Island where, for twenty years, hundreds of farmers invested time and money seeking their fortunes. Few were successful.

Fur Farming [3]

	Fur Farms				No. Animals
Year		County			
	P.	Q.	K.	Total	
1920	213	73	23	309	9759
1925	385	145	40	570	16420
1930	464	181	68	713	20784
1935	426	235	109	770	22473
1940	407	221	106	734	10649

When the big breeders exported breeding stock they destroyed the industry. The market was glutted with pelts from ranches in many countries. The history of P.E.I.'s short-lived experience in fur farming is an example of how industries developed and financed in the hinterland are swallowed up by capitalists in the metropolis.

Despite the high prices paid for pelts and breeding animals few

<u>Fox Farm</u>: *The fox ranch was enclosed in wire which had to be embedded in the ground four to five feet to keep the foxes from digging their way out of the enclosure. (PAC).*

farmers made much money. It took years to regain the initial investment and by that time the industry was on the decline. Those who started late never regained their investments. Many hung on for years after the industry had collapsed. They served as a reminder of an industry which contributed little to the wealth of the community but made a few big producers very rich.

The Great Depression

In his essay "Wages, Prices and Profit", Karl Marx explained how capitalist production moves through periodic cycles. "It moves," says Marx, "through a state of quiescence, growing animation, prosperity, overtrade, crisis and stagnation."[4]

The "boom and bust" nature of a capitalist economy is inevitable, based as it is on a philosophy whose primary goal is the maximization of profits.

The years after the war were years of great speculative investment. Over-investment and over-production led to the biggest economic collapse in history. In 1929, panic gripped the New

York stock exchange. Speculators rushed to sell their shares before they became worthless. New York's panic soon spread throughout the capitalist world.

Production slowed down, first for lack of investment capital, then for lack of markets. Buyers could get no credit, factories came to a halt and unemployment soared.

In Canada, 200,000 people were out of work. Thousands of men, women and children were on the verge of starvation. On the Prairies, farmers were destitute because they could not sell their wheat. Foreign investment was recalled and markets for raw materials dried up. Canada was among the countries hardest hit.

As the chart below shows, living standards in central and western Canada had risen rapidly during the boom of the late '20's. The plunge was dramatic, catastrophic.

The Maritimes, being on the extreme fringes of the hinterland, had not experienced the same boom. Times became harder but they had always been hard.

As the chart indicates, at the peak of the '20's boom per capita

A Lumber Mill: *Ive's mill, one of the many mills where tree logs were sawed into lumber. (PAPEI).*

income in the Maritimes just reached the low point of the plunge in Ontario and British Columbia during the depths of the depression in 1933.

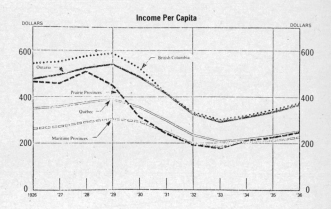

In 1930, the federal government under Conservative Prime Minister, R.B. Bennett, voted $20,000,000 for job creating public works projects.

In 1931, workers at the Estevan, Saskatchewan coal mines went on strike. When they were fired on by the RCMP, workers across Canada were stirred. Sympathy strikes were called in mining camps throughout the West. Workers from Halifax to Vancouver demonstrated, went on strike and organised new unions. Single workers in Vancouver headed for Ottawa in the famous "On to Ottawa Trek". As they travelled across the west their numbers swelled and by the time they reached Regina they were in the thousands. In eastern Canada thousands waited to join. But in Regina, as trekkers gathered at an open air meeting, the RCMP opened fire again. While most of those from the west did not reach Ottawa, a large contingent from the east did march on parliament hill.

In western Canada, new political parties were created. J.S. Woodsworth founded the Co-operative Commonwealth Federation (CCF) in 1932. The left-wing CCF demanded greater public control of the economy through government planning, public ownership of all health services and financial instituions and a more equitable distribution of wealth.

In 1934 William Aberhart founded the right-wing Social Credit Party in Alberta. Social Credit advocated that the government print money and distribute it as dividends to stimulate the economy. When tried in Germany after World War I this produced such extreme inflation that it destroyed the German economy.

The depression left its mark on the Island. Workers at the Davis and Fraser Meatpacking plant in Charlottetown had their wages cut from $17 a week to $12 a week. They could provide for their families only by working overtime. Some men worked as many as 20 hours a day when the opportunity came their way. The only workers not to take pay cuts were the members of the Labourer's Protective Union which, throughout the thirties, maintained pre-depression wage levels.

The prices which farmers and fishermen were paid for their products were low at the best of times; the depression drove them even lower.

Price of Farm Products [5]

Product	Unit	1929	1930	1931	1932	1933
Wheat	bushel	$ 1.59	$ .80	$ .85	$ .75	$ .86
Oats	"	.65	.32	.29	.24	.30
Barley	"	1.02	.60	.51	.40	.50
Buckwheat	"	1.06	.65	.50	.45	.55
Mixed Grain	"	.75	.40	.33	.30	.40
Potatoes	"	.95	.39	.18	.24	.27
Hay & Clover	ton	12.29	11.00	9.00	7.50	8.00

Value of Fish Sold [6]

1929	$1,297,125
1930	1,252,478
1931	1,078,901
1932	988,919
1933	842,315

Although farmers had very little money they always had food and a place to live, and few lost their land.

Loading Potatoes: *Each autumn potatoes were loaded into ships for export at a number of the small ports surrounding the Island coast. (PAPEI).*

For the fishermen, matters were worse. The price of fish declined, and the men turned to the co-operative movement and the fishermen's unions for relief.

The Co-operative Movement

The first fishermen's union was formed in Tignish in 1925. Its success led to the eventual establishment of more than a score of others. The second union was formed in Alberton in 1930 but it was not until the depression had eased that these two were joined by others. In 1935, 4 new unions were formed, 7 in 1936, 6 in 1937, only one in 1938. Six were established in 1939 and a further 2 between 1940 and 1942. Twenty-eight unions in all in fishing communities from one end of the Island to the other.

The first official recognition of co-operatives came with the passage in the Island legislature of the Credit Union Societies Act in 1936 and the Co-operative Association Act in 1938. All co-operative activities before that time were either informal or operated through joint-stock company legislation. The Co-operative Association Act guaranteed open-membership and democratic control and made it difficult for the co-op's to turn into capitalist-style ventures benefiting only the shareholders.

The thrust behind the expansion of the co-operative movement in the thirties had originated in Antigonish, Nova Scotia. Priests at St. Francis Xavier University, led by Father Cody, had encouraged the setting up of co-operatives to counter the growing influence of Communism. The Communist Party was making steady gains in the coal fields of Cape Breton and eastern Nova Scotia where workers were building strong working class unions under the leadership of men like Jim McLachlan. Telling the workers that "under capitalism the working class has but two courses to follow: crawl or fight",[7] McLachlan advocated the revolutionary overthrow of the bourgeoisie and the rule of the proletariat.

Historically, the servants of the bourgeois class, the priests in the Antigonish movement preached that the co-operatives would bring the same results as those endorsed by the Communists but without violence. In the end, by not confronting capitalism, by not recognising that true co-operativism and capitalism cannot co-exist, the Antigonish movement failed. The co-operative movement was but a stop-gap measure. It helped alleviate the worst abuses of capitalism without changing the basic social structure.

The co-operatives did give the rural people of P.E.I. an opportunity to work together to improve their situation. The leading figure in the movement in the 30's was J.T. Croteau, of Acadien descent, who came from the United States in 1932. Supported by the Catholic Church he modified and applied the Antigonish programme to the Island. By organising study groups in depressed communities he taught people how to set up and manage their own co-ops.

The early co-operatives had been set up and run by the farmers and fishermen as production marketing organisations. Croteau built consumer co-ops.

Between 1939 and 1974, 76 co-operatives were incorporated under the Co-operative Association Act. 40 are still in business.

In addition to retail co-operatives, Croteau set up Credit

Unions. As in the time of the Farmer's Bank, the chartered banks would not lend money to people who were "a poor credit risk". The credit unions provided loans at interest rates far below those offered by the banks. 72 credit unions were started on the Island. Today 13 remain.

Because the co-operatives operated in a capitalist economy they were compelled to conduct their affairs largely with capitalist economic rules. This meant they tended to occupy the marginally profitable areas of the economy. Their activities, in fact, helped stabilize monopoly capitalism. By concentrating on consumerism, the later co-ops failed to attack the root causes of economic oppression and gave the illusion of a better life. They have had the effect of prolonging the oppression of the mass of workers and farmers under the capitalist economic order.

In spite of its ultimate result the co-operative movement once again demonstrated the people's will to fight for collective self-improvement.

Chapter Notes

1. quoted from *Cummings Atlas*.
2. *Prince Edward Island Magazine*, October, 1902.
3. Andrew Hill Clark, *Three Centuries and the Island*, Toronto, U of T, 1959, p. 151.
4. Karl Marx, *Wages, Prices and Profit*, Peking, Foreign Languages Press, 1969, p. 69.
5. *Canadian Annual Review* for years 1929 through 1933 inclusive.
6. *Ibid.*, same years.
7. ――――, "People's History of Cape Breton", Halifax, 1971, p. 48.

22

World war
and aftermath

World War II (1939-1945)

After World War I, Germany was destitute. The imperialists who had defeated her were ruthless in demanding that she pay for the damages done by the war—demands that were impossible to meet.

After 1918, the Social Democrats came to power in Germany. The political philosophy of social democracy is to eliminate the worst evils of capitalism; to make the rich a little less rich and the poor a little less poor, without altering the basis of the social structure. (The New Democratic Party in Canada today.)

In 1933, when Adolf Hitler was "elected" chancellor he established massive state controlled corporations. He assumed dictatorial powers and set about to eliminate his chief enemy, the Communists.

The German industrial complex had not been destroyed during the war but huge war payments and massive inflation had made it impossible for German capitalists to accumulate the capital needed to expand. Hitler stopped the war payments and embarked on the conquest of Europe on the pretence of freeing the citizens of the fatherland.

In 1936, he aided General Franco in setting up a fascist dictatorship in Spain and forged an alliance with the Italian fascist leader Mussolini and with imperial Japan.

Britain's Prime Minister Chamberlain and French President
Daladier tried to appease Hitler by allowing him to take the
Rhineland in 1935, Austria in 1938 and Czechoslovakia in 1939.
The Soviet Union's Joseph Stalin urged Britain and France to
form a united front against fascism. When his proposal was rejected he bought time to prepare for war by signing a non-
aggression treaty with Germany in August 1939.

Now Hitler was in command. Temporarily free of the Soviet
threat, he invaded Poland in September, Japan invaded Man-
churia and the world was at war.

Canada declared war on Germany on September 10, 1939. The
Canadian parliament voted 100 million dollars for war operations.

By 1941, Germany had conquered Denmark, Norway, Holland,
Belgium, France, Hungary, Rumania, Yugoslavia and Greece. As
the master of Europe Hitler broke the non-aggression pact with
the Soviet Union, Germany's single largest threat, and invaded
Russia.

In December 1941, Japan attacked Pearl Harbour and the
United States was brought into the war. In the same year, Germany and Italy invaded North Africa.

In Canada, Mackenzie King's Liberal government proclaimed
compulsory military service in 1941—for the defence of the country only. In April 1942, he held a national plebiscite asking the
Canadian people to answer "yes" or "no" to the question: *Do you
agree to free the government from all obligations resulting from
previous promises restricting the methods of mobilization for
military service?* The people answered "yes" and King
claimed conscription for overseas service.

During the war Canadian soldiers again distinguished themselves as brave and effective fighting men. On August 18, 1942,
the British sent 6,100 soldiers, of whom 4/5 were Canadian
shock troops, in 253 boats to test the German defences on the
French coast at Dieppe. When they landed on the beach they were
cut down by German machine gun fire. After two hours of
slaughter the British commanders decided that the defences were
indeed formidable and ordered a retreat. 2,752 of 4,963 Cana-

dians were killed and 617 wounded. In the interests of the metropolis, even the lives of the hinterland people were expendable. When the allied forces invaded Normandy in 1945 the Canadian contingent made the deepest penetration into German occupied territory.

The War Economy

The war brought great prosperity to Canada.

Tanks, warships, synthetic rubber and other war materials were manufactured by Canadian industry which received millions of dollars in low interest loans and grants from the government. The government raised the money by selling Victory Bonds to the Canadian public. War production wiped out unemployment. For the first time women were brought into the factories and mines on a large scale to replace the men who entered the armed services.

As in World War I, the greatest benefits went to the industrial centres of Canada. But P.E.I. was important as a supplier of foods. It was also strategically important for aircraft flying the North Atlantic. Bases were built almost overnight at Mount Pleasant, Summerside and Charlottetown. The demand for food increased farm and fish production. The hungry thirties were over and the Island's jobless went to war.

After the War

The war cost Canada 21 billion dollars plus 4 billion dollars in grants and material aid given to Britain.

Between 1918 and 1939, the United States surpassed Britain as the greatest imperialist power in the world. Increasingly the U.S. looked to Canada for new resources and as a place to invest capital. Because Britain had been shattered during the war, the U.S. now had a free hand in Canada.

As U.S. capital flowed into Canada to develop primary industries, Canadian raw materials were sold at shamefully low prices (iron ore at 1 cent a ton) to be processed in the United States, then sold back to Canadians as finished products.

The federal government acted as caretaker and supplied the

infrastructure—roads, railways, etc.—necessary to move resources from the hinterland. For this service it received donations to its party funds. The services were paid for by taxing the Canadian people.

Because the Maritime region is not an important resource area, few roads were built after the war. Not until 1970 was work started on a modern highway between New Brunswick and Montréal. Instead, the Macdonald-Cartier Freeway was built from Montréal to Detroit.

After the war, J. Walter Jones, a gentleman farmer, headed the Liberal government of P.E.I., a government still dominated by the Island merchants. Since 1900, a few of the merchants had become millionaires. Among the most notable were Austin Scales, owner of an electrical company and of the Island Fertilizer Company; Carl Burke, former owner of a local airline, Maritime Central Airways, (since sold and renamed Eastern Provincial Airways); the Holmans, DeBloises and Carvells in the wholesale-retail business. This group dominated the political life of the Island and saw to it that their class interests were paramount.

Trade Unions

After the flurry of activity in the early decade of the century, the only unions to survive were the national railway unions and the Labourers' Protective Union. However, workers did try to organise. Around 1917, employees of the Davis and Fraser Packing Company in Charlottetown were being made to work an extra hour without pay. The workers wanted to organise, but, as Leo Dowling relates, "Nobody wanted to be head of it, so 15 or 16 [workers] got together and went out to the woods ... got a sheet of paper and everyone put their name down in a circle [on a document demanding pay for the extra hour]. There was nobody at the head of us." [1] When their demand was made [it was mailed] the workers received pay for the extra hour.

In the late '20's the packinghouse workers organised and affiliated with the American Federation of Labour. Their union collapsed during the thirties. Throughout its short life it used the LPU hall and received encouragement and help from the longshoremen.

About the same time, the truckers who transported coal in handcarts from the docks to local merchants organised the Truckmen's Union, again with the help of the LPU. They affiliated with the AFL initially but later became independent. Their union collapsed when motor trucks took over the moving of coal in the late '30's.

During this period the LPU, Truckmen and railway workers, continued to organise the annual Labour Day Parade and Sports Day which brought together workers from all over the Island.

In 1942, Mr. Best, an organiser for the Railway Union, and Art Gormley, the President of the LPU, started to organise support for a Workmen's Compensation Act. They talked to the government, often stopping Cabinet Ministers in the streets. After much persuasion a Compensation Act was passed in 1948.

In 1944 the packinghouse workers organised again, this time with the United Packinghouse Workers of America (UPWA). A year later the workers at Maritime Electric organised with the International Brotherhood of Electrical Workers (IBEW).

Chapter Notes

1. Leo Dowling,
   From a taped interview in the possession of the author.

23

The merchants' last stand

J. Walter Jones—Would be Dictator

On August 26, 1947, UPWA called a strike against Canada Packers, Swift Canada Ltd. and Burns Packers in Moncton, Toronto, St. Boniface, Moose Jaw, Edmonton and New Westminster. By September 11, the strike was national in scope and workers at the Canada Packers Charlottetown plant set up picket lines, the first major strike in P.E.I.'s history. The union demanded 92 cents an hour all across Canada. For Charlottetown workers this would be a 32 cent an hour increase.

1947 Hourly Wages for Packinghouse Workers[1]			
Charlottetown	60 cents	Moose Jaw	74½ cents
Moncton	72 "	Regina	74½ "
Montreal	74 "	Prince Albert	74½ "
Toronto	77½ "	Edmonton	73½ "
Winnipeg	73½ "	Vancouver	82 "

On September 26, government representatives from all provinces except P.E.I. and B.C. met in Toronto to discuss appointing a national conciliator.

The Island government decided to deal with the strike in its own way. Premier J. Walter Jones offered the workers a 50-cent bonus for every hog killed if they would go back to work at the old pay pending a national settlement. Although some of the union members in Charlottetown were willing to accept this offer, the national union rejected it.

On the day following Jones' offer, his government made an order-in-council which nominally turned the plant over to the government. On September 30, the plant, manned by a few "scabs", re-opened. Some farmers crossed the picket line to work but most left when they realised the significance of the struggle. Because it was the first major organised strike on the Island many people didn't know the purpose of a strike or a picket line. The plant barely kept going. Only 8% of the normal daily number of hogs was being slaughtered.

On Tuesday, October 9, the government declared the strike illegal and issued the following statement:

> WHEREAS the government of this province by an Order-in-Council dated September 27, 1947, took over the operation of the plant and other facilities of Canada Packers Limited of this province;
>
> and WHEREAS the packinghouse workers of UPWA Local 282 have gone out on strike against Canada Packers Limited;
>
> and WHEREAS the said packinghouse workers have refused to go back to work despite an offer of 50 cents per hog;
>
> and WHEREAS both parties to the dispute which led to the strike are directed from Toronto, Ontario, and by the expropriation action of September 27, 1947, Canada Packers Limited are no longer an employer within the meaning of the Trade Union Act;
>
> and WHEREAS the said Trade Union Act does not bind the crown to bargain collectively or to recognise any trade union;
>
> and WHEREAS the individual workers are on strike against Canada Packers Limited and not on strike against the crown;
>
> and WHEREAS the people of the province both producers and consumers are adversely affected by such strike action;
>
> COUNCIL DID AND DOTH ORDER that all existing strike action against the present operation of the said plant is declared to be illegal and DO AND DOTH ORDER that appropriate proceedings be taken to terminate such strike action, whether the same takes the form of picketing or otherwise, which interferes with the employees in their

operation of said plant under the direction of the crown.[2] The government-appointed controller, Horace Wright, tried to get union men back to work by saying, "a worker can be employed by the government and still be on strike against Canada Packers."[3] The government's claim to be running the plant was a lie. The general manager and the office staff of Canada Packers were still at the plant. The government was simply acting to break the strike.

Jones' claim that he acted to help the farmers was also a lie. Across the province, farmers had held several meetings and publicly supported the workers, stating that Island workers should not get 12 cents an hour less than workers at Moncton. Jones' real feelings about the farmers were revealed a year later. When a group of them presented a brief to the legislature asking the government to do something about marketing, Jones yelled at them, "You would not be here if you were good farmers. If you were real farmers you could hardly afford to be away from your place."[4]

Jones blamed the workers for the government's failure to establish secondary industry. "We cannot get industry here unless workers take lower wages,"[5] he said. He suggested that "If labourers were not satisfied to work eight hours a day for pay and four hours out of loyalty to his employer then they should seek employment elsewhere. . . . You must forget this eight hour a day shift," he said, "let Nova Scotia have it—not here. If we get our backs up we may pass a law outlawing all unions in the province. If union men don't like to pitch in like the big majority of our people here . . . then I say let them go somewhere else."[6]

The truth was that the only way to bring industry to this outpost of the hinterland was to offer incentives. Jones' incentive was a compliant, low-paid work force, unorganised if possible.

In October, UPWA workers across the country agreed to go back to work. In P.E.I., Jones refused to "return" the plant to Canada Packers until the scab workers were guaranteed permanent jobs. Union members refused to agree with this condition and the government continued to run the plant.

In March 1948 Jones implemented his earlier threat when the

government amended the Trade Union Act and made it illegal for a union on the Island to be affiliated with a body outside the province.

George Saville (fifth Kings) said "the present government will see that no outsiders come in here and tell local labourers when they are going to work, who they are going to work for, and what they are going to work for." [7]

Jones is Overruled

But by now there was a new balance of power. The working class was organised and had to be recognized.

The federal government, backed by the Canadian Congress of Labour, forced Jones to rescind the amendment to the Trade Union Act, making it clear that if he refused to do so, the federal government would disallow the legislation.

In defending the government's position, Horace Wright, in desperation proclaimed that the action "had been taken at the time to keep communism out of this province." He charged that "a communist agent from Toronto had been in the province until after the bill was passed ... hoping he would be able to take over." [8]

The strike was over, Canada Packers got their plant back and the 75 year reign of the Island bourgeoisie was coming to an end. The best efforts of the bourgeoisie's last great defender, J. Walter Jones, were not enough to save it.

Chapter Notes

1. *Charlottetown Patriot*, September 27, 1947.
2. *Charlottetown Guardian*, October 9, 1947.
3. *Ibid.*, same date.
4. Mackinnon, *The Life of the Party*, p. 112.
5. *Patriot*, October 30, 1947.
6. *Ibid.*
7. *Ibid.*
8. *Ibid.*, February 20, 1948.

24

New rulers
gain control

Industrial Plunder, the beginning ...

Modern imperialism is Capitalism developed to a point where
monopolies play a decisive role in economic life. The monopolization of the economy had been in process in the industrial heartland of Canada since about 1920. The '50's witnessed the en-
croachments of monopoly capitalism on independent farmers,
fishermen and businessmen.

The influx of U.S. capital and the development of monopolies
brought a great increase in consumer goods to central Canada.
The Island people demanded a share. However there was a
porations develop in ways that are of greatest benefit to their organisations. In Canada this meant developing the industrial
region between Montreal and Hamilton; the sub-metropolis from
which the Canadian hinterland was exploited. If industry was to
move to P.E.I. it had to be compensated for locating so far from
the industrial centre whence it came. It made no attempt to
accommodate to the Island's rural society. Indeed it demanded
that rural society be adjusted to meet the needs of the intruder.

Rather than use public funds to develop industries run by the
citizens of the province and meeting the needs and using the resources of the island, Jones and his successors paid the companies
to come. The word went out: "Years without taxes!" "Lucrative

Fishing: *Above, aboard a fishing schooner in an Island harbour. (PAC).*
Below, the wharves and fish houses at Rustico. Note the lobster pots in
the background stacked ready for use when the two-month lobster seas-
son arrives. (PAC).

government grants!" "We guarantee that you will be satisfied with the profits!" "If your return is not high enough, we'll give you another grant!" Naturally they came!

In the fishing industry draggers were used for the first time and canneries were built to process the larger catches. Two plants were built in Souris; one locally owned, the other owned by a United States' company.

In 1953, Heeney Frozen Foods opened P.E.I. Frosted Foods in Sherwood. The President of Heeney Foods was William Heeney who lived in Rockliffe Park, the exclusive residential colony of the Ottawa compradors. Heeney was enticed to the Island by a multi-million dollar government grant and a long tax concession.

Farmers were told that they would have a new market for their products and for the first few years they grew cash crops such as peas, broccoli and brussel sprouts which were sold to the company. Then the company bought its own land. The farmers and their sons became hired labourers working for Heeney at wages as low as 65 cents an hour.

Canada Packers and the potato dealers were quick to take advantage of the new developments. Farmers were told by the government that they must expand; to expand they needed money; they didn't have any. Canada Packers and the dealers came to their aid with almost indecent haste.

Canada Packers offered hog producers all the feed they needed on contract credit. They didn't have to pay until the pigs were ready for market. But then, by the terms of the contract, they had to sell the pigs to Canada Packers at whatever price they were offered. The company deducted the cost of the feed from the payments to the farmers. If what was left was less per pig than the farmer needed to cover his production costs, he was told to raise more pigs to earn more money.

Many farmers accepted the company's offer of "help". They signed new contracts, borrowed money to build more buildings and sold the market-ready pigs at Canada Packers' price, a price which often only covered the cost of raising the pigs and paying the interest.

Potato dealers offered potato growers fertilizer, insect sprays and even the seed on credit. When the potatoes were ready for market they had, by terms of the contract, to be turned over to the dealer to pay the bill. There were 112 licenced dealers on the Island but 90% of all the potatoes were handled by 12 of them. One Island farmer who sold to an American dealer summed it up when he said: "Who takes the beating? the P.E.I. farmer. Who makes the profit? the U.S. dealer."[1]

Chain of Exploitation in the Food Products Industry			
	Farmers Fishermen	Produce Company	Company Worker	Wholesaler Retailer
Activity	Harvester Producer	Packer Middleman	Packaging Labelling	Seller
Productive Labour	70%	0%	30%	0%
Profits taken	3%	35%	2%	60%
Social Class	Petit-bourgeois	Bourgeois	Proletariat	Bourgeois

Potato Marketing Board

In 1950, the P.E.I. Potato Growers Association came under attack by the private dealers. In 1953 the Association established the Potato Marketing Board as a selling agency and dealers were relegated to assembling and shipping the potatoes to market.

The dealers found it more profitable to make arrangements with big potato brokers with whom they bartered for bigger markups. They were not satisfied with fixed income under the Board's arrangements.

A plebiscite was called to determine the future of the Board. At first the question was to be a straight "Do you want a marketing board?" The Board was to be the only marketing agency. Alex Matheson, a Charlottetown lawyer who replaced Jones as premier in 1953, came to the dealers' rescue when it became apparent that the plebiscite would carry in favor of the Board.

Matheson argued that no one in a free society should be compelled to sell his product to a specific dealer. Raising the cry of communism he stated: "As long as I am premier of this province there will be no compulsory anything." The question on the plebiscite became two questions: "Are you in favor of the Marketing Board?" and "Are you in favor of compulsory marketing?"

In the vote the first question got an overwhelming **YES!**; the second, a resounding **NO!** Matheson and the dealers were successful. The whole idea of the Board was to find good markets and offer farmers uniform prices throughout the year. Without compulsory selling to the Board the dealers had only to offer higher prices than the Board to corner the market. It was hard for unorganized farmers who needed money on a day to day basis to think about the future. When there were bills to be paid they sold to the highest bidder. Under these conditions the Board did not even try to operate.

Federal Provincial Relations

The provincial premiers of the Maritime region were continually seeking more money from Ottawa—the so-called "Equalization Payments" made by the federal government to the poorer provinces. In 1956 Matheson and the other Maritime premiers appealed to Ottawa to increase the equalization payments. The federal Liberals, now under Louis St. Laurent, refused.

With no help from Ottawa, the Island Conservative leader, R. R. Bell, started to talk about Maritime secession from Confederation. No one took him seriously. For R. R. Bell it was merely a desperate effort to turn the electorate against the Liberals so that his party could get at the trough they had been excluded from for over twenty years.

In 1957 the national Conservatives, under John Diefenbaker, took office in Ottawa. Diefenbaker was less than enthusiastic about the rapid trend to U. S. ownership and alarmed at the diminishing British interest in Canada. He discouraged U. S. investment and made great speeches about the glorious monarchy and the British tradition of John A. Macdonald. He won the support of voters in the Maritimes and the Prairies by initiating federal 'assistance programmes' to these areas and finding markets for wheat.

In 1959, under the Atlantic Provinces' Assistance Programme, P. E. I. got a 2½ million dollar grant and a proportionally larger

Oysters: *These shell fish are one of the delicacies taken out of the Island waters. Most of the oysters are exported. Above: oysters are scraped from the bottom of the shallow water by the use of the long-handled tongs, then put in the small boat to be taken ashore for grading, below. (PA-PEI). The hammer-like instrument in the fisherman's hand is used to separate and clean the individual oysters. (Canadian National Railways).*

share of the federal income tax.

By 1959 Islanders had had enough of the Liberals. Walter R. Shaw, who had been Deputy Minister of Agriculture under the Liberals, led the Conservatives to power for the first time since 1935. He promised great development and lots of aid from "our friends in Ottawa."

Chapter Notes

1. *The Charlottetown Patriot*, January 18, 1964.

25

Conservative Premier — liberal gifts

The new government began an energetic "development" programme; a programme designed to bring big business and monopolization to the Island. The first steps were taken when Hartwell Daley, a United States newspaperman working for the Summerside Journal, was appointed Director of the Research Division of the Department of Industry and Natural Resources in 1961. Since the main resource considered exploitable was the beauty of the countryside and the miles of clean beaches, Daley immediately undertook to build an industry on this by bringing in more tourists.

First, he initiated the Community and Recreational Development Programme (CRDP) under which people in areas considered prime for tourist development were encouraged to take a ten week course in community and regional development as unpaid volunteers. The course was by correspondence and based on similar courses that Daley had been involved with in the United States.

Second, after being suitably trained, volunteers were sent out to do economic surveys of their area. Then the volunteers gathered in committees to decide what they were going to do. And finally, they went to work to "improve" their area. A number of the projects received grants under the federal Agricultural Rehabilitation and Development Act (ARDA) programme.

Tourism As Industry

Tourism is not an industry. It produces nothing. However its effects on the social and cultural life of the inhabitants of a tourist region are devastating. Tourists come to a place like P.E.I. because it is un-polluted and un-scarred by industry, because it is quiet, because there is an absence of the awfulness of urban sprawl. Their coming brings with it the social ills from which they are attempting to escape.

Tourism in P.E.I. is seasonal (just over 2 months). The jobs it provides are seasonal too and of little social value. They are far from personally satisfying. Tourism is no basis for a stable economy. Fully half the income from tourism leaves the Island to buy goods and services used by the tourists. Non-residents inflate the prices not only of shore property but of farm land and building lots as well, making it next to impossible for young farmers to get started. The situation encourages corporate farming and destroys the traditional economy.

Tourism reinforces a colonial hinterland economy. It undermines the local economy. Tourism is a product of capitalist society and is one of its most abominable manifestations.

The CRDP programme initiated by Daley was the basis for a major expansion in tourism. Most of the work done was in the area of recreation—fixing up parks to make them more attractive for the anticipated flood of tourists, making handicrafts to be sold to the tourists, etc. Most of the volunteers who did the work to attract the tourists received none of the benefits. The beneficiaries were to be resort owners, gas companies and merchants. Each summer, as increasing numbers of tourists invaded the province, the local residents were pressed into service as chamber maids, guides, tour directors, waitresses, gas jockeys, store clerks, lifeguards and housekeepers. For most, wages were pitifully low, in some cases as little as $25.00 a week. The bulk of their incomes came from their ability to pamper, cajole, praise and grovel for tips. Each year thousands of tax dollars were used to promote the trade and for grants to resort developers. Taxpayers receive little in return except inconvenience and loss of money which results from not being able to use the roads. The tourist trade makes the Island a "Coney Island" with neon signs, night clubs, pollution, and congestion. The quiet countryside becomes a fairground.

The Industry Robbery

The Shaw government spared nothing trying to attract industry. To the new industries went sizeable start-up grants and later further grants were made when the companies complained about insufficient returns on their investments. The P.E.I. Industrial Development Council (IDC) was set up to administer the grants. Two consulting firms from the United States and one from Norway were brought in to study the situation and make recommendations.

Over a period of time, a pattern of events became discernible. A company would come to the Island and receive a grant from the provincial government. After a few years in production, there would be the threat of closing. An additional grant would be made. Finally, like good poker players who knew when to cut and run, the plant owners would declare bankruptcy and leave.

The most blatant example of corporate robbery concerned two industries in Georgetown—Gulf Garden Foods and Bathurst Marine. The latter was to build fishing ships to be sold to the former, to be used to bring fish catches for processing.

Jens Moe, a Norwegian who went out of business at Bathurst, New Brunswick, proposed to the IDC, together with Uniconsultants of Norway, a scheme to build a shipyard and a processing plant. The ships, said Moe, would bring fish to the plant which would employ hundreds of workers and bring prosperity to Georgetown.

Moe and friends received an initial grant of $750,000 before Uniconsultants dropped out of the scheme. Moe found new partners, Premium Iron Ore Ltd., a United States' investment and holding company sent to develop natural resources in Canada.

Together they built Bathurst Marine.

Moe then signed a contract with Findus Products, a Swiss Co., which would buy the products of the yet-to-be-constructed Gulf Garden Foods. Contract in hand, he went to the IDC for another grant—this time for $1,000,000.

Industries Established 1953-1966 [1]

Company	Location	Grants to 1966	Activity
*Gulf Garden Foods	Georgetown	$2,800,000	Fish-food Processing
*Bathurst Marine	Georgetown	400,000	Shipbuilding
Langley Food Packers	Montague	1,500,000	Vegetable-Food Processing
*Seaman Bros.	New Annan	500,000	Potato & Food Processing
*P.E.I. Frosted Foods	Sherwood	n/a	Food Processing
*Island Packers	Summerside	355,000	Fish Processing
Cromwell Farms	Cardigan	110,000	Potato storage & Packing
Morell Packing	Morell	n/a	Fish Processing
Judson Packers	Summerside	160,000	Meat Packing
*Island Flax Co.	Freetown	150,000	Flax
Stella Maris Atlantic Fish Co.	North Rustico	225,000	Fish Processing
Canada Industries	Roseneath, O'Leary	n/a	Agri-chemicals
Fraser Valley Frosted Foods	Montague	1,000,000	Food Processing

*Companies since gone out of business or bankrupt.

n/ Not Available
Not a complete list

Another U.S. Company, Commercial Marine International, botched the plan for Gulf Garden and new consultants were brought in. The final consultants' bill was $2,335,342. Their designs for the plant were inadequate and the operation was a disaster. To cover up, the government poured in more money. Ships built at Bathurst Marine lay at anchor, rusting in Georgetown Harbour because there was no plant to process the fish.

The contract for refrigeration went to United States owned Lewis Refrigeration (Canada) Ltd. for $603,349.00 although another company had bid $393,636.00. The President and General Manager of Lewis Refrigeration, Cyril Davies, was appointed to the same offices at Gulf Garden.

When the plant finally started up with a lower than planned capacity because of design defects, it had cost over $6,000,000, paid for the most part out of public funds. An additional $4,000,-000 went to keep it in operation until it was closed down in 1967.

Despite this fiasco, the Shaw government's generosity with the taxpayers' money continued. As a benefactor to the corporate welfare bums, P.E.I. had few equals.

The International Unions

By the mid 1960's the Island's economy was controlled by the new foreign companies. Island merchants, who had once ruled supreme, were fighting to stay alive. Big retail chain stores like K Mart, Dominion, Loblaws and Eatons established themselves and threatened to crowd the smaller Island merchants out of business. Their cries of distress fell on deaf ears; the government had new masters.

As more and more Islanders, the sons and daughters of once independent farmers, fishermen and merchants, became labourers in the new industries, the United States unions came to organise them. The Island government changed the labour laws to bring them more in line with those of other provinces. Unions with well known names like the International Brotherhood of Electrical Workers, IBEW, International Association of Machinists, IAM, the United Steelworkers of America, USA, all giants of U.S. labour, organised the small plants on the Island.

To justify their presence and intimidate their members, John Brown, an executive of IBEW, told the workers "that P.E.I. locals are a drain on the national union. Moreover," he continued, "this is quite in order as Canadian unions are a drag on their [United States] headquarters." [2] Between 1962 and 1973, United States unions made a net profit of over 183 million dollars from their Canadian branches. Quite a drag, but not on the American unions.

The Farmers

Under a marketing board set up by the Shaw government, a levy of $0.01 was to be made on each bag of potatoes sold. The money would be used for promotion and marketing research. The farmers refused to pay the levy and the case went to the Supreme Court.

Andrew McRae, Minister of Agriculture in the government that was pouring out $10,000,000 to Jens Moe blithely commented: "The potato industry is notorious for expecting the government to do everything for it. I am not asking for more money to encourage the industry until the industry starts to play a more co-operative role." [3]

In 1966, Shaw called an election. The Liberals under their new leader, Alex Campbell, a Summerside lawyer and son of former Liberal premier Thane Campbell, blasted the Conservatives for the Georgetown robbery—without calling it a robbery. Islanders were not sure whether to elect Campbell or not. They were fed up with the promises of comprador politicians, promises which always ended up costing them money. On election day 15 members were elected from each party. But there had to be a deferment in the election in one of the dual ridings because of the death of a candidate. The Conservatives were still alive.

The government appointed one of the Conservative candidates to the Cabinet and moved into the Eastern Kings County riding—where the election had been deferred—with most of the road building and paving equipment on the Island. The electorate was not to be bribed. In defiance they returned two Liberals to the legislature. During the election campaign one woman in derision erected a sign which read **PLEASE DON'T PAVE MY LAWN**.

Because of the Island electoral system the Liberals gained a majority in the legislature and formed the next government.

Campbell took over as Premier with the Georgetown scandal as a legacy. He promptly poured more money into Gulf Garden to keep it going. Bathurst Marine was taken over by the Fisherman's Loan Board and continued to build ships.

Campbell appointed a Royal Commission to investigate the Georgetown situation. After the commission reported and the

Dual Ridings

Two member ridings are a relic of the days when one member, called a councillor, was elected by property owners and the other, an Assemblyman, was elected by all voters. Under this system it was possible for an elector to vote in every riding where he owned property. The system was abolished in 1962 but two member ridings remain.

facts made public the plant was closed down. Jens Moe had absconded with a large part of the $10,000,000 that the government had poured into the operation in a little over three years.

Campbell blamed the former Conservative government of Walter Shaw for the whole affair and set about convincing the people that no such scandal would happen under his government.

Population 1969   109,000

Chapter Notes

1. *Financial Post*, June 26, 1965.
2. *Ibid.*, September 8, 1962, p. 11.
3. *Ibid.*, March 14, 1964, p. 7.

26

The plan

Researched and Planned Exploitation

The Campbell government set about a development research programme. The premier told the people, "We have lacked confidence in our own ability to seek opportunities for development."[1] The truth was that the people had sought opportunities, only to be robbed of them. Now the people were to pay for research into even better ways for them to be exploited.

By 1967, over half a million dollars had been spent by the Shaw and Campbell governments in numerous studies. Still more experts came *to give the people confidence.*

In September 1967, Russian experts were brought in to demonstrate new land clearing techniques and Campbell announced that "the Russian activity has sparked interest on the part of the United States equipment makers and we have invited some of their agents here to demonstrate their machinery on selected projects."[2]

While all the planning, research and demonstrations were going on, the federal government designated the whole Island an underdeveloped area. This, according to Campbell, was a great decision because the provincial government could take charge of planning with the assistance of Ottawa.

Ottawa established the Fund for Rural Economic Development (FRED). "The great promise of FRED," said Campbell, "is that

it is designed for the province to use as a gap-filler between existing plans and the development of an overall, comprehensive plan
to cope with our problems over the long haul."[3] FRED provided
funds for yet more research with "experts" coming to tell Islanders what must be done if the Island was to prosper.

P.E.I.'s economic problem is really quite simple. Situated as it
is on the fringe of the hinterland in a colonial capitalist economy,
its fate under capitalism is always to be exploited, never to be developed. Since planners and researchers never openly acknowledge
this situation, planning and research, as means to developing the
Island for the good of its inhabitants, are exercises in futility.

But D.W. Gallager, General Manager of the Economic Improvement Corporation (EIC), a government agency, set up to administer the flow of federal money and to direct research, asserted
that "P.E.I. doesn't have the people capable of managing the
plan"[4] so "education" was necessary. The experts went to all
parts of the Island to study the situation and to "educate" the
people to prepare them for the plan which the government promised would lift the Island out of its economic misery.

To carry out the new education plans, schools were built and
construction boomed. In 1966 and 1967, over 125 million dollars
were spent in construction of schools, hospitals, government faci-
lities and university expansion.

Outside investment continued. Alvin Keenon, from Wood-
stock, N.B., a potato dealer operating twelve farms in New Brunswick, bought 1,500 acres of land in New Zealand, near Souris, and
built a 2,300 foot runway to accommodate an air shuttle service
between his interests in P.E.I. and N.B.

The Imperial Tobacco Co. bought 425 acres of land to grow tobacco.

The Island's principal potato dealers and the processing
companies bought land to expand their operations. Twelve
dealers handled 90% of the potatoes shipped from the Island.

This centralization resulted in small farmers and fishermen
being squeezed out. They became labourers for the companies
and large landholders. They experienced a renewal of the leasehold tenure system that had oppressed their forefathers a century

before.

Average size of farm 1911	85 Acres
Average size of farm 1971	171 Acres

As more and more people joined the ranks of wage earners, American unions moved in again. The government through the Department of Labour set up courses in industrial relations, based on successful techniques developed in the United States, designed to provide the employers with contented docile workers.

Canadian Agriculture—the Federal Plan

In 1970, the Federal Government's Task Force on Agriculture recommended that Canada's agricultural industry become a resource base for United States agri-business. The report was simply a detailed plan for imperialist absorption of the industry. In part it recommended that "The primary specific trade goal of Canada should be to negotiate a free trade Continental Market with the grains, oilseed, potatoes and some fruit and vegetables."[5] It further recommended that "Younger non-viable farmers should be moved out of farming through temporary programmes of welfare, education and provision of jobs in other sectors of the economy. Older farmers should be given assistance to assure that they have at least a "liveable standard of living."[6]

In P.E.I. the government, under the guise of development, had been moving ahead rapidly to achieve these same goals. Of Walter Shaw it might be said that he acted impulsively out of a desire to put on a good show for the purpose of winning elections. No such charge can be laid against Alex Campbell. From the day he took office he embarked on a programme to wrest control of the land from the small farmers and place it in the hands of large farmers and agri-business.

The Development Plan

For two years after Campbell became premier, the much-talked-about Development Plan was always "six months away" or "about to be signed". When the results from the studies were finally compiled and a plan drawn up by the Economic Improvement Corporation it took another year of negotiations and redrafts before the federal government approved it.

Although the plan was signed on March 7, 1969, a full ten months less a week before the Task Force on Agriculture submitted its report on December 31, 1969, its recommendations dovetailed perfectly with those of the Federal Task Force. Obviously, the federal government knew what the Task Force was going to say long before it said it. The year of negotiations was a stalling tactic to bring the Island plan into conformity with the federal plan. Both were federal plans. Many of the experts who had worked on the P.E.I. presentation quit in anger and disgust because the final version bore little resemblance to what they had conceived for Island development.

But Campbell was ecstatic. He announced the plan as a self-help scheme. Assistance was to be offered only where there was a reasonable chance of significant economic return. It was intended to be a make-work programme. It called for spending $725 million over a fifteen year period; two thirds of it was earmarked for education.

In January 1970, Campbell, faced with the problem of not being able to find a director who would do what he wanted, decided to take the job himself. He created the Department of Development and appointed himself minister.

Chapter Notes

1. *Financial Post*, November 11, 1967, p. 20.
2. *Ibid.*, November 11, 1967, p. 20.
3. *Ibid.*, November 11, 1967, p. 20.
4. *Ibid.*, March 23, 1968, p. 25.
5. ——————, "Canadian Agriculture in the Seventies". Report of the Federal Task Force on Agriculture, Ottawa, 1969, p. 433.
6. *Ibid.*, p. 432.

27

The plan
in operation

From the beginning the plan had three main objectives: (1) to consolidate farm land and increase the number of large, corporate holdings, (2) to run an education programme designed to meet the needs of a tourist centre (3) to transform the Island into a playground for tourists.

Land Development: One of the first agencies set up was the Land Development Corporation (LDC). Its purpose is to buy land from farmers who wish or can be induced to sell. Farmers over sixty can sell their land to the LDC at a price agreed on by the agency. As part of the deal, married farmers are pensioned off at $228.88 a month ($181.76 single) and given the use of the house and one acre of land for as long as they live.

By 1971, the LDC had acquired 25,000 acres of land, a total of 175 farms. The LDC sells the land to what it considers 'viable' farmers.

The Lending Authority was set up to lend money to farmers to help them improve their operation. It put many farmers deeply in debt which then allowed the Lending Authority to foreclose and collect the land. One farmer, who signed his letter "a little guy", wrote to the editor of the Guardian to say, "Out of the goodness of their hearts they did actually give a group of small farmers $45,000" (a year's salary for one of the experts). "Six months later they did not show a profit, so they are going to take the sucker away from them."[1]

For the first two years of the plan, nothing was done in the agriculture and fishing sectors except for the activities of the LDC and the Lending Authority. However, millions of dollars were poured into other sectors.

Tourism: An article in *The Financial Post* shows us the image of P.E.I. promoted by the government.

> That's the way Prince Edward Island is, a kind of dreamy never-never land that most of us haven't known since childhood—unsophisticated, slow-paced, and satisfying, where the sun shines every day and tomorrow's problems never arrive.[2]

The Maritime Magazine, *The Atlantic Advocate*, intones the same propaganda:

> Prince Edward Island still maintains the charm of a century ago—blessings of fresh ocean air, a pure uncrowded environment. It is a place of leisure, an area of contentment, a holiday haven.
>
> The soil is rich and the landscape predominantly green, giving the Island province a fairy-land appearance.
>
> The outstanding historical event in the Island's history occurred in 1864 when Canada's first confederation conference was held in Charlottetown.[3]

This image is encouraged by the government—"a place of fun." The name "Holiday Island" has superseded historically significant names like Minagoo, Abeweit and The Island. Even the ferries which ply the straits were painted a disneyland green and named "Holiday Island" and "Vacationland." The green was a bit too gross and the ships were re-painted white but the names remain.

To further transform the Island into a holiday centre for affluent tourists, over a quarter of a million dollars was spent to build golf courses at Brudanell and Mill River. To accompany the golf course at Brudanell a recreation-restaurant complex was constructed. This complex, an American style night club complete with 'sex kittens,' was operated by Kitten Lounge Systems Limited, a United States' operation which is a competitor of the Playboy clubs. The "little guy" who wrote to the Guardian asked, "If the quarter of a million dollar, 250 seat restaurant does not show a profit in the first six months, will it also be closed?"[4] The kitten show was later cancelled because of the cries of indignation which arose from the Island people.

By 1971, 500,000 tourists invaded the Island in the summer months—outnumbering almost five to one the 110,000 residents many of whom became the servants of the "visitors." In 1974, the number of tourists had climbed to 625,000.

Tourism turns the Island into a zoo each summer, turns a living culture into saleable artifacts and gives tourists' needs precedence over residents' needs. An advertisement in the Charlottetown Guardian in June 1973 instructed Islanders to be "sidewalk ambassadors."

The government hired Project Planning Associates of Halifax and Toronto as consultants. They made the following observation in their report:

> We believe it will be increasingly useful to think of the whole of Prince Edward Island as a park. As this view becomes generally accepted, the Island will be seen in a new and important context. Every part of the Island will be appraised in terms of its international tourist and recreational potential. Every activity will be considered as a function of a living park, where a variety of socio-economic activities take place.[5]

If this advice is followed, and there is no doubt that this is the government's intention, then the local people must be convinced that this is what they want. Hence the 'education' component of the plan.

In early 1970 the federal and provincial governments decided that 12,000 acres of land in the East Point area were to be a federal park—a national park.

Dr. Lorne Bonnell, Minister of Tourism, announced that where farmland fell within the park, farmers could continue farming it. He was clearly lying since the agreement between the two governments reads: " . . . Prince Edward Island will deliver possession of these lands to Canada and ensure that any and all interests therein of whatsoever nature and kind lying with any person or persons are terminated."[6] On April 10, 1970 a memorandum was circulated by R.V. Blakeley of the Dept. of Development to his staff members on the subject of "social motivations in the East Point Relocation Area." He suggested that the Rural Development Council, a body set up by Island clergy to create attitudes of self-sufficiency and self-reliance, could be used to convince the people that they wanted the park they didn't want. The memorandum specifically instructed that open meetings were to be avoided. It set as its objective "to persuade as many people as possible that the change is for the better, prior to the issue becoming crucial."[7]

Fortunately for the people the proposed agreement was stolen and distributed to the East Point Area with a map indicating that only the farms of the Minister of Agriculture, Dan MacDonald, now a federal cabinet minister, and other influential families were to be exempt. The crisis had come rather more quickly than the government had wanted and the park plan was withdrawn, at least temporarily. The RDC is yet another example of an organisation, born as a popular instrument of the people, coming under the control of the bureaucrats and then being used against the best interests of the people.

Despite the resistance of many Islanders to the continued expansion of tourism, the government's propaganda machine never ceases in its efforts to convince Islanders that it is good for them—that it creates employment, brings more of the good life to the people.

Average Weekly Wages and Average Hours of Work [8]					
	HOURS				
	under 20	*20 - 39*	*40 - 49*	*40*	
	(Number of Employees)			Total	% of Total
under $80	316	1474	379	19	2188	31.93
80 - $100	4	278	1856	65	2203	32.15
$100 - $130	7	90	942	177	1216	17.74
$130 - $200	5	76	764	233	1078	15.73
$200	3	30	101	32	166	2.42
Total	335	1948	4042	526	6851	99.97
% of Total	4.88	28.53	58.99	7.67	100	

The employment created by tourism is largely part-time.

64.08% of workers in tourism earn $100.00 a week or less. 66.66% of them work more than forty hours a week. These are the working conditions created by tourism. These are the jobs that bring the good life! No wonder it's hard for the government to convince the people that tourism is good for them.

Education: Under the plan more money was to be spent on education than anything else. Islanders must be educated, said the government, if they were to take advantage of the new developments. In 1969, the two universities, St. Dunstan's, a catholic institution, and Prince of Wales College, a public institution, were amalgamated to become the University of Prince Edward Island. Holland College, a technical institution, was established in Charlottetown.

Despite the continued objections of many Islanders, education at the elementary and high school levels has been centralized in consolidated schools far removed from their natural communities. This, probably more than anything else, has served to break up the established community structure of the Island, based as it was on the district schools. Now, instead of more than 100 local school boards, there are only seven—five in the rural area and one each in Summerside and Charlottetown. These boards are administered by bureaucrats out of touch with the local people. Decisions are made, not by the people directly concerned, the parents, but by civil servants in the Dept. of Education.

Thousands of students attended high school and university. They graduated to seek jobs in an economy where winter unemployment annually runs as high as 20%. Many leave the Island to find work elsewhere.

Nevertheless, the government went ahead with the plan and added the slogan "taking government to the people." Offices were set up in different areas of the province to talk to, not with, the people. Funded by Ottawa, each office has a receptionist called an "intake worker." As told to the Financial Post, "the intake worker diagnoses what programme or service representative the visitor ought to see then summons a guide, or a 'Primary Helper,' to shepherd the subject from interview to interview, with explanatory footnotes offered along the way."[9]

Programmes like this and organisations like the Rural Development Council were to receive the responses and reactions of the rural population—supposedly to permit changes to be made in the plan. In fact they were designed to do two entirely different things. First they gave the government the opportunity to anticipate and circumvent popular opposition to its objectives. Second, they provided a propaganda network to convince the people that tourists, corporate farms and agri-business are what they need.

Under the terms of the plan the Island government has the responsibility of having the plan accepted. This is its role as the local comprador—carrying out the essential local task which would be impossible for Ottawa or Washington to do. P.E.I.'s role is clear. In fulfilling the needs of the metropolis it is to be a rest centre, a place of beauty and quiet to which the more affluent in the metropolis can from time to time retreat and refresh themselves for meeting the horrors of their cities.

The effect on the people of the Island is considered only in so far as it will be necessary to train them in their place in the grand design. The traditions and culture of the Island will be supplanted by the "culture" of the metropolis. The people are told that their rich rural traditions are passé, that if they are to prosper they must adopt the new cultures and the new economic trends. After 200 years of neglect, imperialism has a use for P.E.I.

One Islander wrote to the Guardian to ask "Should taxpayer's money be spent to have darling sex kittens display for the exclusive dalliance of wealthy male tourists? Are we going to allow our Island to turn into the kind of place where only wealthy sportsmen and gamblers feel at home?"[10] By their actions the Campbell and Trudeau governments say "yes". The people of the Island by their actions say "no".

Chapter Notes

1. *Charlottetown Guardian*, To the Editor "A Little Guy", February 16, 1971.
2. *Financial Post*, May 2, 1970, p. 16.
3. *Atlantic Advocate*, April, 1972, p. 43.
4. *Guardian*, "A Little Guy", February 16, 1971.
5. David Cayley, "Underdeveloping Prince Edward Island; Notes on the P.E.I. 'Development Plan'." Toronto, Development Education Centre, 1973.

6. *Ibid.*
7. *Ibid.*
8. —————, "Tourism Employment Study" Prince Edward Island. A Study of the Employment Impact of Tourism on the Prince Edward Island Economy. Charlottetown, Queen's Printer, 1976, p. 25.
9. *Financial Post,* October 30, 1971, p. 39.
10. *Guardian,* To the Editor "Discouraged Islander", May 4, 1971.

28

The struggle
— a new stage

When the Plan was signed in 1969 it was announced that the Net Provincial Product (NPP) would increase by an average of $150 million a year and Per Capita Income (PCI) by close to $1,000 a year. Promising great things, Campbell won re-election in 1970 with one of the largest majorities in the history of the province.

However, within a few months it became clear that the increases in NPP and PCI were being distributed among that small percentage of people who were involved in the tourist trade, agribusiness or corporate farms.

A letter to the editor of the Guardian, on February 9, 1971 from a farmer, shows clearly the real direction of the development plan:

> The primary producers are the people who produce the wealth of the country, namely, the labouring man, the fisherman, farmer, miner, and lumberjack. All others are engaged in the following services and professions. The classifications are—the primary producers, the dark collars, the servicing personel, the blue collars and the white collars, the bureaucrats, the bankers, university counselling personel, economists, financiers, . . . the irony of this classification is that in the competition for money, the last are first and the first are last.
>
> In Russia prior to the communist revolution of 1917 the bureaucrats or non-productive people absorbed such a large proportion of the economic earnings of the country that they

became economic parasites . . . bringing on the uprising of the proletariat.[1]

In February of 1971, U.S.-owned Seabrook Farms in New Annan, which acquired P.E.I. Frosted Foods Ltd. of Sherwood in 1969, declared bankruptcy. The government stood idle as the President of the company had equipment moved to another plant in Québec to keep it from being seized, even though the plant had been taken over by the government. When farmers asked the Campbell administration to guarantee $200,000 in Seabrook contracts the Premier let them know that the government had no responsibility to growers whose contracts were defaulted by Seabrook. Later, the angry demands of the farmers forced Campbell to honor the contracts. While the government had to be pressed to take responsibility for its people, Seabrook had been bailed out by grants and loans until, when it went bankrupt, it owed the government $2,000,000. The government, which ordered a commission of enquiry into the Georgetown fiasco when it was opportune to embarrass its Conservative opponents, refused even to answer questions about Seabrook. While pouring millions into the American owned Seabrook, Campbell refused to give assistance to the producer-controlled Morell Co-op when it suffered a disastrous fire.

The people were angry and showed it in letters to the Guardian in the winter of 1971. People from all classes attacked the government. A writer from Miscouche expressed well the feelings of Islanders:

> . . . I think we all better use our heads and not try to turn our beautiful farm homes and lands into beaches. It is not everyone on P.E.I. who can make a living in 2 months out of 12. How are we to survive? I suppose we could approach the development council and they would give us a $125.00 a month pension, and put us all in a field with a nice board fence . . .[2]

A meeting of potato growers was called in Tignish to establish a farmer controlled marketing agency "for the purpose of effectively and orderly marketing of a quality controlled product packed under strict supervision in designated warehouses or packing centres as opposed to the several inactive, inadequate and detrimental organizations* now in existence."³

The National Farmers Union—NFU

When it became clear that government policy was to get farmers off the land or under the control of agri-business, they joined their own organisation—the NFU. The NFU had been founded in Saskatchewan to combat the encroachment of agri-business. As one P.E.I. farmer later put it "we started to move when we formed our own organisation completely removed from government influences and concerned with the welfare of farmers."⁴

Demands of the NFU in P.E.I.

1. That the government negotiate in good faith, the solution to farm problems, with the National Farmers' Union.

2. That the P.E.I. government immediately cease enacting agricultural legislation complementary to the Federal Task Force on Agriculture's recommendations.

3. That the P.E.I. government cease enacting legislation and implementing regulations that discriminate against farmers.

4. That legislation be enacted that will abolish vertical integration [forcing farmers to contract with agri-business for the sale of their products].

5. That legislation be enacted that will abolish corporate farming.

6. That truck registration fees be drastically reduced.

7. That farmers be allowed to use marked gas in farm trucks.

8. That long-term, low-interest loans be provided to farmers.

---

*These included the P.E.I. Potato Producers' Association, P.E.I. Potato Dealers' Association, P.E.I. Potato Marketing Board and the Department of Agriculture.

Bill 55: *Above, Premier Campbell addressing the demonstrators who came to protest the government's imposition of Bill 55. Below, note that many of the placards demand justice for the farmers. (Private Collection).*

<u>NFU Demonstration:</u> *(1) Roy Atkinson, the national president of the NFU, addresses the farmers. (2) One of the placards carried during the demonstration. (3) Tractors slow up traffic on the main route to Charlottetown. (Private Collection).*

<u>Road Block</u>: *Tractors block the access road to the ferry terminal at Borden. All traffic was tied up for six hours. (Private Collection).*

When the government refused to talk with the farmers' representatives, NFU members instructed their officials to organise a demonstration march on the provincial legislature.

Public Order Act—Bill 55

The government took a page out of Prime Minister Trudeau's book and enacted their own mini War Measures Act. The act, drawn up in collaboration with the R.C.M.P. detachment on the Island, provided for the prohibition of certain public gatherings (gatherings considered undesirable by the government or the R.C.M.P.). A reason to introduce the Act came when a group in Charlottetown organised a rock concert called Junction '71. It was passed through three readings in a single three hour sitting of the legislature on April 6, 1971. There was one dissenting vote.

Public opposition to the Bill was swift and militant. On April 7, 2,000 people marched on the legislature to demand that the Bill be rescinded. 1,500 of the marchers were farmers. They called for immediate reductions on licence fees for farm trucks, tax free gas for farm trucks, subsidised interest on farm loans and higher taxing of non-resident land owners.

Following the demonstration the farmers organised a picket at the provincial administration building. They gave away food to draw attention to their problems. Pressure from the farmers and the active support of many people forced the government to meet with NFU leaders. Campbell announced that Bill 55 would be rescinded in the fall session of the legislature. The people of the Island had proved that the government could not run roughshod over their determined opposition. They had scored a victory.

When the NFU leaders met with the cabinet, most of their demands were turned down but they were led to believe that something would be done about farm vehicle licensing and tax free gas. The NFU gave the government until the end of July to confirm that belief.

Workers and Farmers Unite

During the summer of 1971, the government notified unions that labour legislation passed in the last session of the legislature would be implemented. However, the government was anxious to see certain contracts signed before the new legislation, which benefited collective bargaining, came into effect. Under the old laws each shop in the IBEW had to take a separate strike vote because of separate certification. The IBEW wanted the new legislation enforced so that all the members would vote as one unit. The union was opposed also to a government decision of August 10th to reject a number of applications for certification.

When the government refused to take action against construction companies attempting to bribe workers to remain outside the unions with $25.00 a week raises, the carpenters' union went on strike. They were joined by the IBEW. The farmers, angry with the government for not meeting their deadline, again instructed their leaders to organise tractor demonstrations. Once organised, the farmers drove hundreds of tractors along the highway to slow up traffic at central points, including the main road between the ferry terminal at Borden and Charlottetown.

The Minister of Agriculture, Dan MacDonald, in an effort to buy time, promised the farmers that Campbell would meet with them. They took him at his word and called off the demonstration. When MacDonald's promise proved to be false, a mass rally for farmers was called in Charlottetown on the evening of August 18th, the same day the certification applications were to be turned down. At the rally union leaders promised to stand behind the farmers and there was talk of a province-wide general strike.

On the 19th, farmers blocked an access road to the ferry terminal. Three farmers, Herbert Stewart, Jimmie Mayne and Wayne Sharpe were arrested and later released after being charged with obstructing traffic. Sometime that day Campbell, through an Order-in-Council, put the new labour legislation into effect. Union leaders reneged on their promise to the farmers and ordered their members back to work. When these leaders, the international union representatives on the Island, had the chance to bring the arrogant government to its knees and win an important fight for both the workers and the farmers they shook hands

Police intervention: (*1*) *R.C.M.P. arrive in a school bus accompanied by road graders from the P.E.I. Department of Highways ready to use force if necessary to remove the tractors.* (*2*) *Armed police, hands on gun butts, demand that the farmers remove their tractors.* (*Private Collection*).

with the government and congratulated themselves on how well
they had used the farmers to get what they wanted.

On the morning of August 20th, Campbell, his deal with the
unions secure, went on radio in a special broadcast to slander the
NFU, hoping to turn the farmers against their leaders. At 1:00
p.m. that afternoon the farmers responded by evading the
R.C.M.P. and driving over 200 tractors onto the road to block the
main ferry terminal at Borden.

Attorney-General Gordon Bennett ordered the R.C.M.P. to
enforce the law and clear the highway. At 7:00 p.m. fifteen
R.C.M.P. patrol cars and a school bus full of additional
R.C.M.P. (some of them soldiers in R.C.M.P. uniforms)—a combined force of 150 police—backed up by road graders from the
Department of Highways prepared to scrape the tractors off the
road.

The farmers, reduced in numbers (many had taken their shifts
and gone home to do farm chores), decided to avoid violent con-
frontation and removed their tractors.

The next day they returned. This time, NFU president Roy
Atkinson was arrested on a charge of conspiracy which was later
dropped. Although forced to leave once again, the solidarity of the
farmers strengthened both their organisation and their determination to fight.

The government, with editorial support from the Thompson-
owned Charlottetown Guardian, told the farmers they should get
a good P.R. man who would direct them to take action which
wouldn't offend the public, more precisely the tourists. But farmers had support from people all over the Island and beyond.
Workers, teachers, small businessmen and university professors
stood behind them. A letter which appeared in the Guardian from
Thomas M. MacLellan very clearly stated this support.

> The present organized effort of the NFU is the most heart-
> ening sign I have seen from our farmers in my lifetime.
>   I was happy to be detained in your tractor parade three
> times in one day: the time spent waiting was only very short
> in comparison to the very long wait the eastern Canadian
> farmer has had to get a decent human living from a life of
> hard work.[5]

Chapter Notes

1. *Charlottetown Guardian*, To the Editor "Farmer", February 9, 1971.
2. *Ibid.*, To the Editor "Disgusted", February 12, 1971.
3. *Ibid.*, "Disgusted", February 12, 1971.
4. —————, From a tape in the possession of the author.
5. *Guardian*, To the Editor "Thomas M. MacLellan", August 25, 1971.

29

The people fight back

Land Ownership and Control

The most significant and alarming change in the Island in the 1970's is the increase in corporate and foreign ownership of land.

Non-resident Ownership of Land in Acres [1]		
October 1970	60,000	4.3%
January 1971	72,000	5.2%
June 1972	84,000	6.0%
October 1972	92,000	6.5%
2000 AD	361,000	25.7%

The above figures do not include land owned by corporate farms, which although legally resident owners, in fact, are not.

One Island resident sounded the warning when he said: "If non-resident ownership continues to accelerate we may reach a time when a majority of our land is owned by people who do not reside in our province, a subtle reversion to the absentee landlord situation of a century ago."[2]

Not only is the land being bought by non-residents but much of it is being taken out of agricultural use. While the farm population decreased from 55,478 in 1931 to 21,130 in 1971, so also did the improved land acreage from 770,000 acres in 1931 to 579,558 acres in 1966. These figures show that not only is land being taken out of agricultural production but farm ownership is concen-

trated in fewer hands. While there are 62% fewer farmers there is
only 25% less land being farmed.

In addition to the decrease in farm land and the increase in corporate and non-resident ownership, two other trends must be recorded.

Non-resident Ownership of Shore Property [3]			
	Miles	*% of Total*	*% of Recreational*
1970	77.7	6.8	12
1971	100.0	8.9	16

Much of the shore property has been purchased by land speculators who never intend to develop it in any way. (See chart below).

Building Permits Issued [4]						
	1968	1969	1970	1971	1972	Total
Summer cottage lots created	652	525	986	979	662	3870
Building permits issued for cottages	71	107	127	118	146	569

Non-resident owners are of two kinds: the many who buy small
lots for summer cottages and the few large land owners. Of the
non-resident landowners in 1972 50.2% owned less than five
acres. The total owned by this 50.2% was less than 1000 acres.
The remaining 91,000 acres were owned by people of whom only
4.6% are genuine farmers.

This pattern of land ownership shows the Island's bleak future
if present trends continue.

1. Increased non-resident ownership
   of large tracts of land
   Increased corporate ownership   =   Corporate ownership of land (Agri-business)
   Decline in farm population

2. Increased summer cottage lots
   Speculation in cottage lots
   Large tourist developments   =   Tourism
   Removal of land
   from agricultural use

As well the "new" industries will be owned and controlled by
non-residents.

What have successive governments done about this alarming situation?

In 1939, legislation was passed requiring that all sales over 200 acres to aliens (non-Canadians) be approved by government. This was lowered to 10 acres in 1964.

Between 1939 and 1964 only one application was presented and it was approved. Between 1964 and 1966, sixteen applications were presented and all were approved. Successive governments have encouraged and approved the sale of land to non-residents.

In August 1972 a Royal Commission was appointed on Land Ownership and Land Use. This gave the government a chance to find out what people were thinking on the pretence that it was concerned about their thoughts.

Campbell's government did block a few sales in 1972. Amid the fanfare of this token action 181 purchases by non-residents were approved in the same year, a total of 1,000 acres including over 16 miles of shore frontage.

Requests and Sales to Non-residents [5]

	1972		
---	Total Submitted	Approved	Denied	No Decision
Canadian	108	84	16	8
American	122	93	20	9
Other	6	4	2	--
Total	236	181	38	17
Shore Frontage sales approved (included in above)	16.019 miles		
Shore Frontage sales denied	2.668 miles		

The Royal Commission presented an interim report in 1973. Both it and the final report concluded that land use is more important than land ownership. This conclusion reinforced the arguments for the plans of the federal and provincial bureaucrats. If the Island is owned by agri-business and non-residents, then they, not the people, will determine how the land will be used. If the people can be convinced that it doesn't matter who owns the land then all their efforts to control usage will be useless.

Support for the land use idea came from the Federation of Agriculture, a government water boy, and the New Democratic

Party, which, like Campbell, talked about opposing foreign
control then acted to foster it. The N.D.P. and the Federation of
Agriculture criticised "discrimination against prospective
buyers."[6] What does this mean? In P.E.I. where, if present
trends continue, over half the good agricultural land will be non-
resident owned by the year 2000, such a criticism is clearly discrimination against the Island people. These pseudo-friends of
the people are really cut from the same cloth as Campbell and
dyed a different colour.

The Civil Liberties Association, the P.E.I. Real Estate Association, and the Conservative Party, argued against any kind of
control. The only strong voices for control of ownership came
from individual Islanders like Mrs. Evelyn Howatt, of Tryon, Alvin Hamilton of Covehead, resident landowners and organisations
controlled by Islanders such as the National Farmers' Union and
the Brothers and Sisters of Cornelius Howett, a group determined
to tell the real story of Confederation in centennial year.

In a letter to the Guardian, Alvin MacDonald paraphrased the
statement of the Real Estate Association:

> Throw the whole thing wide open, let us make hay while the
> sun shines and after all the productive land is sold to non-
> residents, we shall move out and look for greener pastures.[7]

Sixty-three Islanders took time to write briefs and present them
to the commission. Twenty-two more represented organisations.
The anger over the loss of their land and their birthright was expressed strongly. Following are a few statements by Islanders.

Harold McIntyre, Wellington:

> ... The government is forcing Island farmers to borrow
> huge sums of money and it is ruining them as farmers.
> They're borrowing more money than they can ever pay back.
> What we need now is interest free loans to young men who
> want to go into farming ...[8]

A Farmer:

> I'd like to see them (experts) come without their statistics
> just to see what they'd say about the difference which exists
> between what they tell us we're doing and what we can show
> them we're actually stuck with.[9]

Leigh Hodgson, Alberton:

What has all this land usage, etc., got to do with the sale of
shore frontage and farm properties to non-residents?

If Premier Campbell and his government wanted to do
something about the problems, all they have to do is pass
legislation that will make it mandatory for anyone in the
future in order to hold or own shore frontage or farm property on the Island they must be Canadian citizens.[10]
Brothers of the Micmac

> We are told that many [Americans] wish to come here in
> order to escape the social carnage at home; social carnage
> which they helped to create but have not the courage to
> remain at home and cure. We need no such people here.[11]

Control of Marketing

Under pressure from the National Farmers' Union and the public, Campbell was made to revise his position on agricultural
development. In 1972, before the land commission reported, he
proposed a farm loan programme to assist the family farm.

The new programme proposed a fifty-fifty cost sharing agreement with small farmers. A farmer's letter to the Guardian ex-
presses an often heard reaction:

> The farm loan programme is designed to starve out the little
> guy. He has to borrow his share of the cost sharing.
> The 50-50 cost sharing programme is an insidious one
> because the government is "assisting" those who take ad-
> vantage of it into debt.[12]

By now people looked at every new government scheme with a
great deal of skepticism.

Later in 1972 Campbell proposed a Potato Commodity Marketing Board. It was, in fact, the application of Bill C-176, a federal
government scheme opposed by farmers because it would bal-
kanize the Canadian market, setting farmers from different parts
of the country against one another. A plebiscite on the new commodity board was called for August.

Campbell told the Island potato producers that "Island potato
growers ... have a chance to establish an organized marketing
system of their own or completely reject accepting this responsibility."[13]

NFU spokesman, Allison Ellis, had a different view. He said:

"It becomes more apparent that the government is trying to get control of the potato industry, when they keep trying to man- oeuvre farmers into a commodity board the government will be able to manipulate." [14]

It seemed that a majority of Island potato growers believed Ellis. Campbell turned to threats. The farmers had asked that the government maintain control of the former Seabrook plant in New Annan and that they [the farmer] be consulted before any decision was made about its future. The Premier told producers that they would be consulted only if they voted in favor of the commodity board. This was a lie. On July 26, before the plebis- cite, agreement had been made between Industrial Enterprises Incorporated (IEI), (a government agency which replaced the IDC), and C.M. MacLean Ltd. under which MacLean's was given a year's lease on the plant with an option to buy.

On July 28, the Premier denied that any such agreement had been drawn up and said that C.M. MacLean was given use of the plant to process 1½ million pounds of blueberries. He further stated that a decision on the future of the plant would be made after the plebiscite.

On July 29, the agreement between IEI and C.M. MacLean was signed and later approved by cabinet.

On August 19, the potato producers dealt the government a re- sounding defeat by rejecting the commodity board by a vote of 314-240.

The N.F.U. Marketing Plan

During the plebiscite campaign, the N.F.U. had called on farmers to reject the commodity board in favor of a new plan which would make the N.F.U. the bargaining agent for the potato producers. Having committed himself to a marketing plan, Campbell had no choice but to call a new plebiscite on the N.F.U. plan. He announced that the N.F.U. plan would require special legislation which would make the N.F.U. the sole bargaining agent.

The N.F.U. plan was approved by a vote of 415-233. However, the farmers had been misled. After the vote it became clear that their approval meant only that they were in favor of the N.F.U. plan, not the N.F.U. as bargaining agent. The farmers were told a second ballot was necessary to vote for the N.F.U. as bargaining agent.

Both the government and the N.F.U. leaders knew that the vote would not establish a bargaining agent. Both, for their own reasons, chose to leave the impression that this was the final vote. The government wanted to keep a trump card up its sleeve so that if the vote carried in favor of the N.F.U. plan they would have another chance to defeat the N.F.U. The N.F.U. leaders, on the other hand, decided to be opportunist and let things ride. If they won this vote they were sure that they would win the next.

During the legislative session in the winter of 1973 the special legislation was passed and the plebiscite to approve the bargaining agent was called for July.

The N.F.U. went into the vote with great confidence. They had won the last two votes, they were sure that all they had to do this time was to have their name on the ballot.

The government, on the other hand, made full use of their opportunity. All of their agents came out to attack the N.F.U. The President of the P.E.I. Potato Producers Association led the attack. He said: "What you (the farmers) are really being asked to decide is whether you want to place your future, your province's future, in the hands of an organization controlled in Western Canada. What you will lose is your way of life, your Island way of life, founded on the right of man to determine his own destiny." Don Anderson of the inactive Marketing Board and Wallace Wood of the Dept. of Agriculture filled the air waves and newspapers with the same kind of rhetoric.

Not until it was too late did the N.F.U. speak out against this malicious propaganda. The N.F.U. was rejected as bargaining agents by a vote of 440-366 because their opportunism gave some credence to the government's attack. This and their overconfidence led to their defeat. Islanders were reluctant to support an organization which did not tell them the whole truth. Both the government and the N.F.U. were defeated in July, 1973. Both thought they were smarter than the farmers.

The Struggle Continues

In 1974, two Americans who had applied to buy Island land were turned down by the government. They appealed the government's decision to the supreme court of P.E.I. and when the decision was upheld they took the case to the Supreme Court of Canada. After a year of deliberation, during which time all the other provinces came out in support of the P.E.I. government, the Supreme Court of Canada ruled against the appeal. The province's right to determine who could buy land was upheld. This victory established the right of Canadians to control their land. It will be an important precedent in future land battles.

The publicity generated by this case and the many expressions of opposition to foreign land purchases have created an atmosphere which discourages land acquisition by foreigners. In the past two years the rate at which Island land is sold has decreased.

Nevertheless, the government plan to turn the Island into a playground for tourism continues. Yet another study of tourism on the Island was released in 1976. One of the proposals considered but not implemented, was that Island schools adapt themselves to accepting the children of tourists in June and September to allow their parents to come a month earlier and stay a month later. As we have seen, the Island people have fought schemes like these in the past and won. They will continue to fight future schemes of the comprador administrators in Charlottetown to destroy their homeland.

Conclusion

The People's struggle continues.

There is growing opposition to tourism and corporate farming from student, church, community and farm groups. In the fall of 1975, students at the University of P.E.I. boycotted classes in support of low paid maintenance workers. Their action forced the university administration to meet the workers and settle the strike. When the toll booths were constructed at the entrances to the P.E.I. National Park late in 1975 in preparation for collecting proposed park admission fees, nine out of ten were burned down by irate residents unwilling to pay to use their own beaches.

The farmers are once again threatening to put their tractors on the road to block the highways, this time with the growing expectancy of support from fellow farmers across Canada.

The rulers continue to defend themselves against the growing militancy of the people. History is in progress and we hope that this small volume will strengthen the will and determination of the people—the real makers of history.

Chapter Notes

1. ——————, "Report of the Royal Commission on Land Ownership and Land Use", Charlottetown, 1973, pp. 29-31.
2. *Montreal Star*, August 26, 1972.
3. *Ibid.*, p. 59. Also in "Interim Report of the Royal Commission on Land Ownership and Land Use", p. 11.
4. *Ibid.*, p. 35.
5. *Ibid.*, p. 87.
6. *Guardian*, November 24, 1972.
7. *Guardian*, "Letter to the Editor", December 19, 1972.
8. *Patriot*, November 16, 1972.
9. *Ibid.*, same date.
10. *Summerside Journal-Pioneer*, November 28, 1972.
11. *Guardian*, "Letter to the Editor", January 4, 1972.
12. *Guardian*, Letter to the Editor "Harassed Farmer", March 2, 1972.
13. *Guardian*, August 7, 1972.
14. *Ibid.*, same date.

Appendix

Original Landlords	Major Landlords 1860
Lot 1, P. Stephens	Messrs. Palmer, Edward Cunard.
2, J. & W. Hunter	Sir Samuel Cunard.
3, C. Townsend, M.D.	B. Bowring, James Yeo.
4, Adam Keppel,	
5, Edw. Lewis, M.P.	Edward Cunard.
6, W. Croule	
7, J. Montgomery,	R.B. Stewart
8, W. Kilpatrick, B. Dodd	Hon. J. Yeo and others
9, G. Tead, S. Fountenelly	L. Sullivan
10, S. Luthrel, M.P., J. Meteux	R.B. Stewart
11, Col. H. Walsh	Government
12, H. Merre, R. Cathcart	R.B. Stewart
13, Earl of Hertford	Hon. James Yeo
14, Lieut. Gov. DesBrisay	Sir Samuel Cunard
15, G. Carlton,	Government.
16, D. Turres, J. Hayter, J. Tate	L. Sullivan
17, B. Burke, T. Burke	Heirs of Col. Compton.
18, R. Stewart, C. Jamaica, W. Allanby	Misses Stewart & others
19, Gov. Patterson, J. Patterson	A. T. Todd
20, R. Campbell, T. Basset	Sir Samuel Cunard, and Heirs of Penelope Cundall
21, R. Clark	Sir Samuel Cunard.
22, W. Gordon, W. Ridge	L. Sullivan
23, M. Maclean, L. Maclean	D. Hodgson, D. S. Rennie.
24, Col. Lee, F. Maclean	J. H. Winsloe.
25, A. Kennedy, J. Campbell	Small Freeholders.

26, Dr. Stewart, Major Gordon	Messrs. Thompson and others.
27, J. Searle, J.R. Spence	J.C. Pope, R.B. Stewart, and Sir Samuel Cunard.
28, Capt. Holland,	Heirs of George Irving and others.
29, C. Saunders,	Viscount Melville and Lady Georgiana Fane.
30, J. Murray,	R.B. Stewart
31, L. Gov. Desbrisay,	William Douse.
32, W. Young,	Sir Samuel Cunard.
33, L Gov. Desbrisay	J.H. Winsloe.
34, J. Montgomery	Messrs. Montgomery & others.
35, A. Maitland	Heirs of Capt. John McDonald.
36, D. McDonald,	
37, W. Spry, J. Berkley	J.R. Bourke & others.
38, G. Burns,	
39, G. Burns,	
40, G. Burns, G. Spence, J. Mills.	Government.
41, Col. Campbell,	
42, J. McDonald, A. McLeod,	
43, Hon. J. Dormer,	Hon. T.H. Haviland, G. Townshend and Government.
44, W. Fitzherbert, R. Campbell,	
45, W.M. Burt, M.P., J. Calender,	Sir Samuel Cunard and others.
46, R. Campbell, R. Gordon	
47, Colonel Graham, R. Porter	R.B. Stewart.
48, S. Tonchell, J. Cunningham,	Theo. DesBrisay, Capt. Byrne and others.
49, R. Clark,	R.C. Haythorne, Sir S. Cunard.
50, Col. Gladwin, Capt. Inner	Lady Wood, Miss Fanning.
51, Pringle,	Montgomery and others.
52, Capt. Tead, B. Dodd, D. Curry, S. Fountenelly,	James Peake and others.
53, Dr. Hunch, J. Williams, Lieut. Campbell,	Government, Lady G. Fane and Viscount Melville.
54, R. Adair,	Government and others.
55, F. Mackey, H. Finley	Government.
56, Lord Townsend,	Hon. T.H. Haviland.
57, S. Smith, J. Smith,	Government.
58, J. Maugre,	
59, J.H. Mine, R. Cathcot, Capt. Higgins.	Government, and Montgomery.
60, C. Pearce, W. Mackinon,	Government.
61, R. Cumberland,	L. Sullivan.
62, Capt. Spry,	Government.
63, H. Palliser,	

64, Col. Maitland, R. Wright,	Sir Samuel Cunard.
65, H. Owens,	Messrs. Wright and Capt. Cumberland.
66, Crown Lands,	Government.
67, Hon. R. Moore,	Lady Wood.

Note.—The small holdings are necessarily omitted from this list.

Bibliography

The following bibliography is recommended by the author for those who wish to delve deeper into the subject matter of this book. Those books designated G—General are considered to be books for the general reader while others are for more serious study.

Milton Acorn, *The Island Means Minago*, Toronto, NC Press, 1975. G

Harry Baglole and David Weale, *Cornelius Howatt: Superstar*, Charlottetown, 1974. G

Harry Baglole and David Weale, *The Island and Confederation: The End of an Era*, Charlottetown, 1973. G

J. Murray Beck (ed.) *Joseph Howe: Voice of Nova Scotia*, Toronto, Carleton Library No. 20, McClelland and Stewart, 1964.

Léandre Bergeron, *The History of Québec: A Patriote's Handbook*, Toronto, NC Press, 1971. G

Pat Bird, *Of Dust and Time and Dreams and Agonies: A Short History of Canadian People*, Toronto, 1975. G

J. Henri Blanchard, *The Acadians of Prince Edward Island, 1720-1964*, Québec, 1964. G

Francis W.P. Bolger (ed.) *Canada's Smallest Province: A History of Prince Edward Island*, Charlottetown, Centennial Commission, 1973. G.

Francis W.P. Bolger, *Prince Edward Island and Confederation, 1863-1873*, Charlottetown, 1964.

John Bartlet Brebner, *North Atlantic Triangle*, Toronto, Carleton Libary, McClelland and Stewart, 1966.

Benjamin Bremner, *Memories of Long Ago: Island Scrap Book*, Charlottetown, Irving, 1932. G

James M. Cameron, *Pictou County's History*, Pictou County Historical Society, 1972.

Duncan Campbell, *History of Prince Edward Island*, Charlottetown, 1875.

Lorne C. Callbeck, *The Cradle of Confederation*, Fredericton, N.B., Brunswick Press, 1964.

Helen Jean Champion, *Over on the Island*, Toronto, Ryerson, 1939.

Andrew Hill Clark, *Acadia: the Geography of Early Nova Scotia to 1760*. Madison, University of Wisconsin, 1968.

Andrew Hill Clark, *Three Centuries and the Island*, Toronto, U of T Press, 1959.

Gerald M. Craig, (ed.) *Lord Durham's Report*, Toronto, Carleton Library No. 1, McClelland and Stewart, 1963.

J.T. Croteau, *Cradled on the Waves: The Story of a Cooperative Achievement in Economic Betterment on Prince Edward Island*, Toronto, Ryerson, 1951.

E.N.D. Evans, *Uncommon Obdurate: The Several Public Careers of J.F.W. Des Barres*, Toronto, U of T Press, 1969.

Allan Graham (ed.) *Island Prose and Poetry: An Anthology*, Charlottetown, Centennial Commission, 1972. G

Basil Greenhill & Ann Giffard, *West Countrymen in Prince Edward's Isle*, Toronto, U of T Press, 1967.

Naomi Griffiths, *The Acadians: Creation of a People*, Toronto, McGraw-Hill Ryerson, 1973. G

N.E.S. Griffiths (ed.) *The Acadian Deportation: Deliberate Perfidy or Cruel Necessity?* Toronto, Copp Clark, 1969.

Leslie F. Hannon, *Forts of Canada: The Conflicts, Sieges and Battles that Forged a Great Nation*. Toronto, McClelland and Stewart, 1969.

D.C. Harvey, *The French Regime in Prince Edward Island*, New Haven, Yale, 1926.

D.C. Harvey, *Journeys to the Island of Saint John*, Toronto, MacMillan, 1955. G

Carrie Holman, *Our Island Story*, Sackville, N.B., 1949.

Harold A. Innis, *Essays in Canadian Economic History*, Toronto, U of T Press, 1956.

Edward Ives, *Lawrence Doyle—The Farmer Poet of Prince Edward Island*, Orno, Univ. of Maine, 1971.

Edward Ives, *Larry Gorman—The Man Who Made the Songs*. Bloomington, Indiana Univ. Press, 1964.

Diamond Jenness, *Indians of Canada*, Ottawa, 1972.

Greg Keilty (ed.) *1837: Revolution in the Canadas as told by William Lyon Mackenzie*, Toronto, NC Press, 1974.

F.H. MacArthur, *Legends of P.E.I.*, Charlottetown, 1969. G

D.A. MacKinnon and A.B. Warburton, *Past and Present in Prince Edward Island*, Charlottetown, 1905.

Frank MacKinnon, *The Government of Prince Edward Island*, Toronto, U of T Press, 1951.

Wayne E. MacKinnon, *The Life of the Party: A History of the Liberal Party of Prince Edward Island*, Charlottetown, 1973. G

Rev. John C. MacMillan, *The Catholic Church in Prince Edward Island from 1835 to 1891*, Québec, 1913.

W.S. MacNutt, *The Atlantic Provinces*, Toronto, McClelland and Stewart, 1965.

Malcolm Alexander MacQueen, *Skye Pioneers and "the Island"*. Winnipeg, Stovel, 1929.

Leo P. McIsaac, *Blueprint for Community Progress*, Charlottetown, St Dunstan's University Extension Dept., 1952.

Gustavus Myers, *The History of Canadian Wealth*, Toronto, James Lewis & Samuel, 1972. G

Tom Naylor, *The History of Canadian Business, Vol. 1; The Banks and Finance Capital, Vol. 2, Industrial Development*, Toronto, James Lorimer, 1975. G

G.A. Rawluk (ed.) *Historical Essays on the Atlantic Provinces*. Toronto, Carleton Library No. 35, McClelland and Stewart, 1967.

Alan Rayburn, *Geographical Names of Prince Edward Island*, Ottawa, 1973.

S.A. Saunders. *The Economic History of the Maritime Provinces*, A Report for the Royal Commission for Dominion-Provincial Relations, Ottawa, 1939.

Walter Shaw, *Tell Me the Tales*, Charlottetown, Square Deal, 1975. G

Stanley Ryerson, *The Founding of Canada: Beginnings to 1815*, Toronto, Progress Books, 1963. G

Stanley Ryerson, *Unequal Union: Confederation and the Roots of Conflict in the Canadas, 1815-1873*, Toronto, Progress Books, 1968. G

William Menzies Whitlaw, *The Maritimes and Canada Before Confederation*, Toronto, Oxford Univ. Press, 1966.

Jack Winter, *The Island*, Fredericton, N.B. Fiddlehead Poetry Books, 1973. G

A.B. Warburton, *A History of Prince Edward Island*, St. John, N.B., 1923.

——————, *The Vineland Sagas: The Norse Discovery of America*, Baltimore, Penguin, 1965.

Articles

The following articles were most helpful in my research and are listed here for the convenience of those wishing to do further study.

Margaret I. Adam, "The Highland Emigrants", *Scottish Historical Review* XVI (July, 1919).

Theophilus Blanchard, "Address to the 25th anniversary of St Augustine's Credit Union", South Rustico, 1963.

Bertram Blaquiere, "What Fishermen Can Do: The Story of North Rustico", Adult Education League of Prince Edward Island, 1939?

Helen Jean Chapman, "Isle St Jean and the Seven Years War", PAC XXVI (9), May 1938.

Andrew Hill Clark, "Contributions of its Southern Neighbours to the Underdevelopment of the Maritime Provinces Area, 1710-1867", *The Influence of the United States on Canadian Development: Eleven Case Studies*, Durham, N.C., Duke, 1972.

John T. Croteau, "The Acadian Grain Banks of Prince Edward Island", *Agricultural History*, 29, July, 1955.

John T. Croteau, "The Farmer's Bank of Rustico, An Early People's Bank", *Dalhousie Review*, Vol. 36, Summer 1956.

Margaret Ells, "Clearing the Decks for the Loyalists", *Canadian Historical Association Annual Report*, 1933.

Eugene Forsey, "Some Notes on the Early History of Unions on P.E.I.", *Canadian Historical Review*, Vol. XLVI, No. 4, December, 1965.

D.C. Harvey, "Confederation in Prince Edward Island", *Canadian Historical Review* (1933).

D.C. Harvey, "Dishing the Reformers", *Royal Society of Canada*, Vol. 25, Sec. 2, 1931.

D.C. Harvey, "Early Settlement and Social Conditions in Prince Edward Island", *Dalhousie Review*, January, 1932.

D.C. Harvey, "The Loyal Electors", *The Royal Society of Canada*, Vol. XXIV, Sec 2, 1930.

D.C. Harvey, "The Passing of the Second Chamber in Prince Edward Island", *Canadian Historical Association Annual Report*, 1922.

Robin Hood, "The Denmark of Canada", *Cooperative Marketing Journal*, March-April, 1931.

W.Ross Livingstone, "Responsible Government in Prince Edward Island", Univ. of Iowa, 1931.

Rev. D. MacDonald, "The Scottish Catholics in Prince Edward Island, 1772-1922", *Charlottetown Herald,* 1882.

Frank MacKinnon, "David Laird of Prince Edward Island", *Dalhousie Review,* January, 1947.

Frank MacKinnon, "A Statesman's Centenary Sir Louis Davies", *Dalhousie Review,* Vol. 25, April 1945.

Ada MacLeod, "The Glenaladale Pioneers", *Dalhousie Review,* October, 1931.

Ada MacLeod, "Malpeque", *Dalhousie Review,* April, 1926.

Ada MacLeod, "Travels in Prince Edward Island in 1820", *Dalhousie Review,* April, 1923.

W.S. MacNutt, "Fanning's Regime on Prince Edward Island", *Acadiensis,* Vol. I, No. 1.

J.E.B. McCready, "Traditions of Prince Edward Island", *Dalhousie Review,* July, 1923.

William H. Seibert and Florence E. Gilliam, "The Loyalists in Prince Edward Island", *Royal Society of Canada,* Vol. 4, Sec 2, 1910.

Fred von Dreger, "Anatomy or Adjustment: A Critique of the Rural Development Council as Cadre for Cooperative Democracy in P.E.I." *Abeweit Review,* Vol. II, No. 1, Spring, 1976.

David Weale, "Prince Edward Island and the Confederation Debates", M.A. Thesis, Queen's University, 1971.

A. Gary Webster, "Tignish and Antigonish: A Critique of the Antigonish Movement as a Cadre for Cooperativism", *Abeweit Review,* Vol. II, No. 1, Spring, 1976.

——————————, "The Story of the Cooper Family", *The Maple Leaf,* Oakland, California, April, 1936.

——————————, "St John Island and the Voyages of Cabot", *Royal Society of Canada,* Vol. 2, Sec. 1, 1894.

——————————, *Charlottetown Guardian,* Centennial Issue, 1967.

——————————, "Land Grants in Prince Edward Island", PAC, *Annual Report,* Vol. I, 1905.

Pamphlets

Mary Boyd, "Paradises in the Sun", Inter-Church Committee for World Development Education, Charlottetown, 1974.

David Cayley, "Underdeveloping Prince Edward Island; Notes of the P.E.I. 'Development Plan'." Toronto, Development Education Centre, 1973.

George Frederick Clarke, "The True Story (documented): Expulsion of the Acadians", Fredericton, Brunswick Press, 1965.

Helen A. Lawson, "Colonel John Hamilton Gray and Inkerman House", Charlottetown, 1973.

Arlene MacDougall & Violet MacEachern, "The Banks of the Elliot", Charlottetown, 1973.

Wayne E. MacKinnon, "J. Walter Jones: The Farmer Premier", Charlottetown, 1973.

F.L. Pigot, "John Stewart of Mount Stewart", Charlottetown, 1973.

Mary Stuart Sage, "The Lord Selkirk Settlers in Belfast, Prince Edward Island".

David Weale, "Cornelius Howatt: Farmer and Island Patriot", Charlottetown, 1973.

——————————, "Indians of Québec and the Maritime Provinces", Ottawa, Dept. of Indian Affairs and Northern Development, 1972.

——————————, "Lucy Maud Montgomery", Springfield, P.E.I., Women's Institute, 1963.

——————————, "The People's History of Cape Breton", Halifax, 1971.

Index

St Francis Xavier University 178
St John, N.B. 53, 106
St John's, Nfld. 53
St Laurent, Louis 193
St Lawrence, Gulf of 7, 12, 30, 43
St Lawrence River 10, 16, 30, 127
St Margaret's, 85, 87
St. Mary's Road 105-6
St Peters 85
St Pierre, Comte de 18, 19
St. Pierre & Miquelon 28
Sailor's Hope 74, 98
San Francisco 98
Sark, John 102-03
Saskatchewan, 175, 217
Savage Harbour 4, 19
Saville, George 188
Scales, Austin 183
Scandinavia 9, 63
School Act 1877 133-4
Scotland 14
Seabrook Farms 216, 231
Seaman Bros. 200
Seigneurs 30
Selkirk, Earl of 58
Selkirk, Lord 63, 67, 113
   estate of 100
Selkirk Settlements
   P.E.I. 58
   Ontario 58
   Manitoba 58
Separate Schools 133
Seven Years War 44
Shadegomute 5
Sharpe, Robert 63
Sharpe, Wayne 222
Shaw, Alex 37
Shaw, Walter R. 195, 202-4, 206
   government of 199
Shelbourne, N.S. 44
Shellfish People 2
Sherwood 191, 200, 216
Shipbuilding 63-8, 125, 130
Siberia 1
Small, John 90
Smith, Charles Douglas 58, 69-70
Social Credit 176
Social Democrats 180
Souris 20, 40, 78, 85, 121, 125, 139,
   145, 191, 205
Southport 107

Soviet Union 181
Spain 14, 16, 165, 180
Spanish 8
   Empire 16
Spanish-American War 165
Stalin, Joseph 181
Stella Maris Atlantic Fish Co. 200
Stewart, Herbert 222
Stewart, John 70
Stewart, Peter 47, 49
Stewart, R.D. 126
Stewart, Robert 35
Sturgeon River 20
Sullivan, Stephen 63
Sullivan, William W. 133
Summerside 39, 46, 125-7, 138,
   161, 170-1, 182, 200, 212
Summerside Journal 197
Supply question 71
Swift Canada Ltd. 185

Task Force on Agriculture 206-7
Tasmania 81
Tatamagouche 22, 25
Tea Hill 108
Thirteen Colonies 30, 33, 42, 44,
   46
Thirty Years War (1618-1648) 14
Tilly, Leonard 114-5, 118-9
Tignish 121, 125, 138, 142, 171,
   177, 216
Todd, Thomas A. 108
Toronto 81, 138, 185-6, 188, 210
Tourism 198, 209-12, 227
Townshend, James 73, 74
Townshend, Lord 73
Tracadie 4, 19, 25, 34
   settlement 37
Trades & Labour Congress 143
   convention of 143-4
Trades & Labour Congress
   Convention — 1902 143-4
Trades & Labour Council 143-5
Trade Union Act 186, 188
Trade Unions 142-5, 183-4, 201
Treaty of Paris 28
Tremlett, Thomas 59
Trois Rivières 20, 21, 25
Truckmen's Union 184

252   Index